Contents

YORK NOTES

General Editors: Professor A.N. Jeffares (*University of Stirling*) & Professor Suheil Bushrui (*American University of Beirut*)

Mildred D. Taylor

ROLL OF THUNDER, HEAR MY CRY

Notes by Laura Gray

LONGMAN
YORK PRESS

YORK PRESS
Immeuble Esseily, Place Riad Solh, Beirut.

LONGMAN GROUP LIMITED
Longman House, Burnt Mill,
Harlow, Essex CM20 2JE, England
Associated companies, branches and representatives
throughout the world

First published 1995
Second impression 1996

ISBN 0-582-23765-3

Produced by Gem Graphics, Trenance, Mawgan Porth, Cornwall
Printed in Singapore

Part 1

Introduction

The author

Mildred D. Taylor is a black American writer who was born in the southern town of Jackson, Mississippi, and grew up in Toledo, Ohio, which is in the northeast of the United States. Although she decided to become a writer early in life, she has pursued many other goals and interests in addition to her writing. After graduating from the University of Toledo in 1965 she spent two years in Ethiopia with the Peace Corps, teaching English and History.

When she returned to the United States, she recruited for the Peace Corps before entering the School of Journalism at the University of Colorado. As a member of the Black Student Alliance she worked with students and university officials in structuring a Black Studies programme at the University. After receiving her master's degree, she worked in the Black Education Programme as a study skills co-ordinator. Her life and career show the interest in the consciousness and characteristics of black Americans that inform *Roll of Thunder, Hear My Cry* and her other novels.

General historical background

In order to fully understand *Roll of Thunder, Hear My Cry* some knowledge of the American South, and of the Civil War that raged between the northern and southern states between 1861 and 1865, is necessary. Although the novel is set in 1933 it is alive with a sense of the nineteenth century, both in the geographical setting and in the minds of the characters. The attitudes which prevailed both during the American Civil War and in the period which followed are held particularly strongly by characters such as Harlan Granger and the Wallaces in Taylor's novel.

Historians consider the Civil War an event as significant as the American Revolution, when American colonies rejected British rule and the Declaration of Independence (1776) made official America's status as a country in its own right. The Civil War was a war between the northern and southern states of America. It must be understood that the government of America was, and is, organised in a different way from that of Britain. The United States is formed from a number of states; each state is allowed to have its own laws about internal matters, but there are also 'federal' laws fixed by the President and the Congress which apply to the country as a whole. This mode of government is called a federal government.

America is so large that there are great differences in each of the various states in the way people live, the things they grow, and what is important to them. In the period before the Civil War great cultural differences had developed between the North and the South. The South was an agricultural society, mainly producing cotton, tobacco, hemp, rice and sugar. These crops were grown on huge farms called plantations. The plantations were worked by black slaves who had originally been imported from Africa in the slave trade which began in the seventeenth century. The North was more urban and industrialised, with factories making iron and cloth. In the period before the Civil War two thirds of the country's money was found in the northeast, and New York was a big banking centre.

The people living in the North believed that the slavery they saw in the South was wrong. The Southerners justified themselves, as Mama explains in Chapter 6 of *Roll of Thunder, Hear My Cry*, by claiming that slavery brought the advantages of Christianity to the black people, who were felt by the Southerners to be inferior. The relationship between the North and the South was naturally precarious because the two regions had different interests. The northern manufacturers wanted customs duties put on those foreign goods that they themselves could also make, whereas the southern planters wanted free importation of goods because of their concentration upon the cotton trade with Europe. The South feared that it would always be out-voted in Congress, as the population of the North grew. In 1860, shortly after the election of Abraham Lincoln as President, South Carolina and several other slave-holding states seceded from the Union. They became the Confederate States of America, and wanted to be considered as a separate country. A civil war seemed imminent.

After a Confederate attack on a Federal arsenal at Fort Sumter, South Carolina in April 1861, the Civil War began. The North was chiefly fighting in order to restore the Union, but a secondary aim was to free all slaves, especially as the war progressed. Both sides expected a short war. However, fighting went on until 1865 when eventually General Robert E. Lee, on behalf of the Southern Confederacy, surrendered to the Northern General, Ulysses Grant.

This defeat was followed by a period of racial readjustment which was imposed on the South by the North. This period, known as Reconstruction, only served to make the Southerners feel more separate from the North. Slavery ended and four million blacks were granted the legal and social rights that the southern whites felt to be exclusively their own. Reconstruction lasted from 1865 until 1877. One of the ways in which the white community reacted to the threat of the newly emancipated blacks was by the formation of the Ku Klux Klan in 1866. The 'K.K.K.' was a secret society which aimed to establish white supremacy. The poorer whites in particular clung to southern traditions and maintained their former attitude that black people were inferior.

Following the end of Reconstruction a political and social climate of fear and intimidation for black people began in the South. Racial tension grew, and southern states rejected and reversed the laws that had made black people equal. Between 1882 and 1903 over two thousand black people were lynched in the United States. Many victims were burned alive at the stake, while others were castrated with axes or knives, blinded with hot pokers or decapitated. A proportion of these people were pregnant women and children. In *Roll of Thunder, Hear My Cry* Taylor describes the attacks of the 'night men' on the black community. Mr Morrison's story of Christmas of 'seventy-six' when all his family were killed by night men (Chapter 7) describes an act of brutality that was typical during Reconstruction and for more than fifty years afterwards. There were groups of organised night men right up until the 1950s. Mississippi, where *Roll of Thunder, Hear My Cry* is set, was a focus for continued racial violence for many years.

Literary background

There are many black writers who, like Taylor, choose to explore and exhibit the richness and complexity of the black community. By doing so these writers are helping their own people to achieve a deeper understanding of themselves, and at the same time acting as agents of self-discovery for the nation at large. Both black and white people benefit from a new, accurate portrayal of black people. As a novel aimed particularly at young people, *Roll of Thunder, Hear My Cry* has a special role in helping to forge new images of black people in school literature.

Much modern Afro-American writing confronts the brutality of the slave period. The earliest record of Afro-American literature was that produced by the female slave Lucy Terry, her poetry *Bars Fight* appearing in 1746. These first black writers struggled to create images that presented black people as individuals and as human beings – exactly what the system of slavery attempted to deny of them. The poetry that was written by slaves in the eighteenth century was often not published until the nineteenth century. These early writers were dependent on the generosity of their owners to pay for publishing their works. This was followed by the tradition of slave narratives which carried on into the nineteenth century. These narratives were memoirs by former slaves who wrote about life on the plantations, their suffering and their eventual escape to freedom. The accounts are filled with examples of Negro humour, anecdotes of the deception and pretence the slave was forced to practise in order to ingratiate the master, and expressions of religious fervour and superstition.

Above all, they conveyed a longing for freedom and self-respect. Black slaves sought release from physical bondage in their writing.

Another aspect of black culture was music and folklore, and the stories that were passed down from generation to generation. These were often ignored in white social and literary treatment of blacks who chose to portray black Americans in terms of stereotypes, for example, the happy minstrel or the dependent servant. These stereotypes served to partly justify the beliefs and actions behind slavery and discrimination.

The Civil Rights movement, beginning in the 1950s, changed the nature of Afro-American and American literature. As black people began to claim their right to equality, they rejected passivity and, in some cases, embraced violence. In the 1960s the Black Arts Movement was formed; soon all areas of black literature and arts rejected racism and promoted black independence and nationalism. Radical writings were published, for example the autobiography of Malcolm X (1964) and *Die, Nigger, Die!* by H. Rap Brown (1969). These works defined their writers as the survivors of an oppression which had sought to destroy them and all black people. They were aggressive and political works.

The 1970s witnessed the intersection of the Black Rights Movement and the Women's Liberation Movement. Links between black consciousness and feminism were formed, and as a result many black women began to write about their experiences. An autobiographical element is a common aspect of Afro-American literature, present in family stories, slave narratives and memoirs. Women began to write accounts of childhood and adolescence, chronicling the difficult passage into maturity. Black writers tried to show, without sentimentality, how difficult it was to attain a decent life with the disadvantages to which they were born as blacks. It is to this tradition that Taylor belongs.

A note on the text

Roll of Thunder, Hear My Cry was first published by Dial Press, New York, in 1976. It has been reprinted several times since then. The text used in preparing this guide is the 1988 edition, published by Puffin Books, Harmondsworth.

Part 2

Summaries
of ROLL OF THUNDER,
HEAR MY CRY

A general summary

Roll of Thunder, Hear My Cry is set in the American South in the 1930s,
a period which saw the growth of racial tension and the worsening of
trade and living conditions caused by the period of economic depression
which followed the stock market crash of 1929. The novel is narrated by
nine year old Cassie Logan. Together with her three brothers, Stacey,
Christopher-John and Little Man, she is forced to come to terms with the
issues connected with being black at that time.

The Logan family is headed by the children's grandmother, Big Ma.
They are not like the other local black families who work on white land.
The Logans are peculiar because of their independence and wealth. Uncle
Hammer owns a car like that of the local white landowner, Harlan
Granger. Their mother (Mama) is an educated teacher who holds radical
views. She teaches her black pupils about slavery and about the heritage of
black people. These subjects are not part of the syllabus which is set by the
school board.

Taylor makes us aware that the most significant aspect of the Logans'
independence is the fact that they own their own land. She shows us the
way in which they hold onto their four hundred acres despite the threats
and difficulties that confront them. Papa goes to work on the railroad to
supplement Mama's wages, and he returns periodically, on one occasion
leaving the gigantic Mr Morrison to take care of his family. His provision
becomes all too necessary when white jealousy and hatred accelerates in
the region, leading to attacks on members of the black community by the
'night men'. The Berrys are set on fire for supposedly flirting with a white
woman, and Sam Tatum is tarred and feathered for having dared to suggest
that a white man could have been lying. The Wallaces, who own the local
store, are known to have been responsible for the first act of violence.
Cassie's family, with the support and financial backing of white attorney
Mr Jamison, boycott the Wallace store, choosing instead to acquire provisions in Vicksburg. They are threatened for this act of defiance, and Mama
loses her job. When Papa and Mr Morrison return from Vicksburg they too
are attacked by the night men, and Mr Morrison fights valiantly. Famed for
his spectacular strength, he injures the Wallaces. Papa is shot and his leg is
broken when the wheel of their wagon rolls over him.

The differing conditions and treatment of black and white people are also brought home to both Cassie and the reader on a local level, through a number of episodes that directly affect the lives of the Logan children. Their school is much shabbier than the local school for white pupils. Although the white children do not have as far to walk, they are provided with a bus, unlike the black children. It is this bus that makes the Logan children's walk to school so unpleasant, by covering them with dust or mud depending on the season. They are forever being forced to scramble up the banks of the road, much to the amusement of the white school children and the white bus driver. In retaliation, Cassie and her brothers dig a hole in the road, and fill it with water to make it seem as if part of the road has been washed away by the rain. The children watch as the bus pitches into their trap. To their satisfaction, the vehicle is put out of action for two weeks.

At school, Cassie and Little Man are whipped for rejecting the books that the county has given them. On the inside covers a chart records the condition of the books, their age and the race of the pupils to use them. They are in a terrible condition and have been worn out by white children before they were finally donated to the black school. Mama covers the charts with paper, and this is one of the reasons for which she is fired.

On her trip to Strawberry, the nearby market town, Cassie is surprised to discover that white people have the best positions for stalls in the market and are served first in the Barnett Mercantile. Cassie herself is treated ignominiously by Mr Simms who makes her walk in the road and apologise to his daughter, Lillian Jean. Endowed with the dangerous temperament of her Uncle Hammer, Cassie finds her own way of dealing with Lillian Jean; she pretends to be her friend and learns her secrets, and then beats her up in the privacy of the forest.

The novel therefore tackles two levels of injustice – the terrifying visitations of the night riders which form part of the adult world, and the rooted prejudices of society which are shown in the way in which they affect the children. Cassie has to accept and confront all these instances of injustice. Effectively she has to grow up. She learns that she has to decide when principles are worth defending. The two levels at which racism is depicted, both childish and adult, are united when the Logan children's companion T.J. Avery is wrongfully blamed for the crimes of two white boys. The fate of T.J. forms the climax of the novel.

As T.J. explains to the children when he arrives in their bedroom in the middle of the night, he took part in a robbery that was engineered by R.W. and Melvin Simms, and in which he played only a marginal role. R.W. and Melvin Simms had promised to get T.J. the pearl-handled pistol that he had always wanted, saying that they would pay for it later. Believing them, T.J. climbed through a window and let them into the store. They gave T.J. the gun and then tried to steal the cash box. The owner of the store and his wife came downstairs and the Simms injured them. After being beaten up by his white 'friends' T.J. managed to find his way to the Logan household. The children, on hearing his account of the night's events, go with him to his own home. There R.W. and Melvin, accompanied by a gang of white men, accuse T.J. of the crime. They are ready to hang T.J. there and then and Mr Jamison remonstrates with them without success. A terrible night of violence is only avoided by Papa setting light to their cotton fields. Both black and white unite to quell the flames.

In this novel the issues of land ownership, of principles and the processes of growing up, difficult in any situation, are all set against a backdrop of racial discrimination and dramatic weather conditions. Embedded in the text are serious messages about black heritage and black pride. The reader, along with Cassie, is taught what it meant to be black in 1930s Mississippi.

Detailed summaries

Chapter 1

It is October and the first day of school for Cassie, Stacey, Christopher-John and Little Man. The children walk to school along a dusty road. It is the beginning of Little Man's school career, and he walks slowly, trying to keep his clothes clean. Stacey is preoccupied by the thought of being taught for a year by his mother who is a teacher at the school. Christopher-John whistles as he walks but Cassie is irritable at the prospect of being enclosed within the confines of school.

Cassie surveys the countryside bordering the road. An oak tree marks the extent of the Logan land. Their land is composed of two hundred acres that are without debt and two hundred that are mortgaged. There are taxes to be paid on all four hundred acres. Most of the other local families work on land owned by Harlan Granger. A year after the price of cotton dropped in 1930, Cassie's father set off to work on the railroad. The fact that they own their land is of great significance to the Logan family.

T.J. and his younger brother Claude join them in their walk. T.J. has already failed Stacey's mother's class once, and has returned to repeat the year under her tuition. T.J., after hinting that Stacey might help him cheat in his tests, tells them about the burning of the Berrys that took place the night before. Mr Berry and his two nephews were almost burnt to death, after having been doused with kerosene by a group of white men. The bus from the white school draws near, and all the children scramble up on to the bank except for Little Man, who gets covered with dust. Little Man cannot understand why they don't have a bus. Their walk continues, and they meet up with Jeremy, a white boy whose school term started more than a month ago.

The two schools are described, and the difference of their conditions is made very apparent. The terms of Great Faith Elementary and Second, the school for black children, are arranged to fit in with the cotton harvesting. Some pupils have a three and a half hour walk to school. The school building and its teaching equipment are poor. Cassie is taught by Miss Daisy Crocker in a classroom that is partitioned with curtains, divided between the first to fourth grades. She is reprimanded for not paying attention. When 'new' books are distributed to all the students, Little Man returns his book because it is dirty, then, after having decided to accept it, he suddenly throws it on the floor. He has read a chart that shows that the books were donated to black students only when they were in the very worst condition, unfit for the use of white children. Cassie intervenes, and both children are beaten by the teacher.

Cassie resolves to tell her mother. However Miss Crocker goes to see her first and Cassie overhears their conversation. Mama does not criticise Miss Crocker, but glues paper over the offending charts. We learn that Mrs Logan is different from the other teachers; she is more outspoken and radical in her thinking, having been educated elsewhere. Cassie realises that her mother has understood why she and Little Man felt unable to accept the books.

NOTES AND GLOSSARY:

pants: (American) trousers

cotton field: for many years the United States grew nearly half of the world's cotton. The South is ideal for raising cotton. The climate is warm, there is plenty of rain and sunshine while the plant is growing, and the weather is dry when the plant is ripening. It is planted in spring, and harvested in autumn. Cotton is important to the U.S. economy, and is one of the materials that America trades. Cotton is grown on huge farms called plantations, and before slaves were freed, these plantations used slave labour. The slaves were the descendants of Africans first brought to America in the early seventeenth century. Cassie is picking the last of the cotton in Chapter 2 when she sees Papa

share-cropping families: poor families who work on the land of a white owner. In return for their labour they receive a share of the money that the crop earns when it is sold. As Mr Avery explains in Chapter 9, the 'share' is often used up in the year's purchases, leaving the families with no actual profit

Reconstruction: the name given to the period which followed the Civil War between the northern and southern states of

America. The North won and its rulers attempted to re-shape southern society and give practical force to the emancipation of the black people by offering them political power and the opportunity to become self-sufficient. Reconstruction allowed Cassie's grandfather to purchase their land

Yankee: originally somebody from New England; from the Dutch 'Janke' which means 'little Jan'. The word is used by people in the South to describe anyone from the northern states

virgin forest: a forest in its natural state

mortgage: when property is mortgaged, it is put forward instead of money towards paying a debt or given as security for a debt. If the debt is not paid within a certain time, the property is forfeited

in 1930 the price of cotton dropped: this was one of the features of the economic crisis in which America found itself following the stock market crash of October 1929. By 1932 one out of every four U.S. workers was unemployed, and the whole country began to be affected by hardship and hunger. The period is known as the Great Depression, and its effects extended to the European economy. Only after ten years and Roosevelt's policies did America begin to recover

tidbit: usually used to describe a choice piece of food, but in this case the word refers to a juicy bit of information

stalling around: the way in which T.J. is intentionally delaying telling them what they want to hear. 'Stalling' was originally used in the South to describe a wagon stuck in the mud. T.J. will not let his story move forward

towheaded: a person with whitish or blonde hair, especially a child. This is the first indication of the race of one of the children, and the reader is not yet fully aware that the Logans are black

welts: raised areas on his skin where he has been beaten

Jefferson Davis County School: the school for white children is named after the president of the Confederate states. Davis led the southern states in the Civil War (1861–5) against Abraham Lincoln

Confederacy: America is formed of a Union of states. In 1860 a group of seven states (South Carolina, Georgia, Florida, Alabama, Mississippi, Louisiana and Texas) left the Union to form their own separate country. They were known as the Confederacy. These southern states resented the rules that the government was trying to impose with regard to slavery. They were concerned particularly because the main industries in the South were tobacco and cotton, both of which used large quantities of slaves

American flag: the stars and stripes. The fact that the American flag is put below the Mississippi flag, a part of which is the emblem of the Confederacy, is indicative of the way in which the southern states were clinging to their rebel past

plantations: large farms on which cotton is grown

fall: (American) autumn

nigra: a word used by whites to denote black people, conveying an implication of inferiority

Chapter 2

The children are picking cotton, balanced on high poles, when Cassie spots her father coming home. He has brought with him the enormous Mr Morrison. Mr Morrison has lost his job on the railroad for getting into a fight with some white men. Cassie thinks he has come to protect their family. At church it is announced that Mr John Berry has died. A witness told the sheriff who was responsible for the crime, but she was ignored, and accused of being a liar. Papa announces that the Logans will no longer shop at the Wallace store and he forbids the children to go there.

NOTES AND GLOSSARY:

pecan: a pinkish brown nut that grows on hickory trees

burlap: a coarse canvas

ginned: a process by which the seed is removed from the cotton plant, before it can be made into bales

chiffonier: a movable low cupboard with sideboard top

gas: petrol, or gasoline

That's the nigger Sallie Ann said was flirtin' with her: the noun 'nigger' is one that has aggressive and derogatory connotations. At the time in which the novel is set, the adjectives 'negro' and 'coloured' were acceptable to black people. 'Nigger' was felt to be offensive, as can be seen from Cassie's reaction in Chapter 5

tisked: muttered

bootleg liquor: in the United States during the period of Prohibition (1919–33), alcohol was illegal. It was originally smuggled by people with flasks hidden in their long boots

Chapter 3

The month of October is nearly over. It has been raining heavily and the road to school is muddy. The Jefferson Davis school bus is still splashing the children as they are walking to school, and so driving them up the muddy banks of the road. Little Man continues to be upset by the dirt and by the fact that they do not have a bus. He washes his clothes every night and every day he comes home filthy again. One day the children are on their way to school and make the mistake of descending from the bank. They are all forced off the road by the bus. Little Man is enraged and cries. Jeremy comes to walk with them but they behave coldly towards him. Stacey thinks of a plan to stop the bus from splashing them. That lunch time Stacey, Cassie, Little Man and a reluctant Christopher-John go back to where the bus had forced them off the road. Stacey decides not to include T.J. and Claude as he fears T.J. will be unable to keep it a secret. They dig a hole across the breadth of the road, then fill it with water in order to make it look as if part of the road has been washed away. After school they run back and arrive in time to see the bus getting stuck in their hole. The white children will have to walk for at least two weeks until the bus can be fixed. Lots of them, on getting out of the bus, fall into the large puddle.

That night the children cannot study and keep giggling so Mama splits them up. Mr Avery arrives at the house to tell them: 'They's ridin' t'night' (p. 54). The children are sent to bed and eavesdrop from the boys' room. They are frightened, thinking that the night men's activities have been triggered by what they did to the road. Stacey blames himself. Cassie goes back to bed and Big Ma sits at the doorway with a rifle. Cassie wakes in the middle of the night and goes outside. She sees a line of car headlights that stop at the driveway of her house. Two men get out, seem to decide that it is the wrong house, and then the cars leave. Cassie goes back to bed, terrified.

NOTES AND GLOSSARY:

coddling:	cuddling, with wider implications of indulgence
ifn:	a shortened version of 'if only'
gullies:	ravines created by the flow of water
shoot:	an exclamation of dismay
barreled down:	the bus's movement is given speed and a sense of inevitability by the use of this interesting verb which is constructed from a noun

jus' as burnt as you are: just as annoyed and upset as you are
hickory: a kind of tree, its wood often used for firewood
they's ridin' t'night: the night men are on the roads tonight
caravan: a convoy of cars

Chapter 4

Cassie is not sleeping or eating well. She is scared about what they did to the bus and about the night men. T.J. tells them that the night men tarred and feathered Sam Tatum because he called Jim Barnett a liar. The children are terribly relieved. T.J. pretends to forget his hat and is found in Mama's room looking at her books. On the way to school T.J. produces some cheat notes. Stacey rips them up. T.J. makes another set and passes them to Stacey during the exam. Stacey is whipped by his mother in front of everybody but he does not tell on T.J. After school T.J. runs to the Wallace store, thinking the Logans will not follow him there. They decide to risk a whipping, and Stacey and T.J. fight outside the store. The fight is broken up by Mr Morrison, who then takes them home. On the way he tells Stacey that it is up to him to tell his mother that he has disobeyed her. When they arrive home they find that Mr Granger has been to visit Big Ma. He wants their land because it used to belong to his family.

Cassie and Big Ma go for a walk and stop by a pond. All around the trees are felled and rotting. They were cut down because of threats from Mr Andersen. Big Ma tells Cassie how she and her husband met. Cassie's grandfather, Paul Edward, was a carpenter. He bought some land from a Mr Hollenbeck, who had himself bought it from the Grangers during Reconstruction. The rest of the old Granger land was sold amongst various small farmers, including Mr Jamison, the father of the attorney. After the death of his father 'our' Mr Jamison sold another two hundred acres to Paul Edward. Harlan Granger has been trying desperately to reclaim all the land that once belonged to his family.

Stacey tells his mother that he has been to the Wallace store, without disclosing T.J.'s cheating and trying not to implicate his siblings. The children are all sent to bed. That Saturday Mama takes them to visit Mr Berry. They see the injured man, and understand that the Wallaces are responsible for his pain. On the way home Mama talks to local families about boycotting the Wallace store. It is difficult for the poorer families because they make purchases on credit supplied by the men who own their land, and the credit is specifically for the Wallace store, itself on Granger land. Mama suggests that they might be able to shop in Vicksburg if someone else was to give them credit by backing their signatures.

NOTES AND GLOSSARY:

snippety: snappy, irritable

Yessuh, I guess I is: yes sir, I suppose I am

W.E.B. Du Bois's *The Negro*: written in 1915, this book is a significant text in black literary history. W.E.B. Dubois (1868–1963) was a figure in the Harlem Renaissance, creating the 'new Negro' by discrediting negative stereotypes of blacks in white American literature. That Mama should be teaching this book shows her political ideals. Its subject matter echoes Taylor's hopes for her own novel

clapboard: boards, often thinner at one edge, that are used for making the sides and roofs of houses

checkers: an American word for the game of draughts

Born into slavery: born as a slave, to a mother and father who are both slaves

two years 'fore freedom come: freedom came for slaves in 1865 when an amendment to the Constitution of the United States was passed

the fightin': the Civil War between the Southern Confederacy and the Federal Government

Northern and Southern soldiers: the two sides in the Civil War

'Old South': refers to the established values of the rich landowners

period: full stop, end of sentence

cowtail: this seems to be Mr Turner's version of the word 'kowtow' which refers to the Chinese custom of touching the ground with the forehead as a sign of absolute submission

---

Chapter 5

A week has passed, and Cassie and Stacey are finally allowed to accompany Big Ma to the market in Strawberry, leaving at half past three in the morning. Mr Avery had asked Big Ma if T.J. could come too, to do some shopping for him, and she reluctantly agreed. On their arrival Cassie finds herself disappointed in Strawberry, thinking it 'a sad red place' (p. 88). She is surprised and frustrated to discover that the stalls owned by white people have the prime locations and that they must sell their produce from a poor position. Big Ma goes to see Mr Jamison. Cassie and Stacey, encouraged by T.J., resolve to go and order goods from the Barnett Mercantile. At the mercantile T.J. shows them a pearl-handled pistol that he wants to own. White people are given precedence in the queues, and finally, when a white girl Cassie's age is served before them, Cassie reminds Mr Barnett that they were there first. Barnett tells her to get out of the store. Cassie leaves. Confused and angry, she bumps into Lillian Jean Simms, Jeremy's sister. Lillian Jean tells her to apologise, which Cassie does, but she refuses to walk in the road as Lillian Jean tells her to. Lillian's father intervenes and knocks Cassie off the pavement, twisting her arm in the process. Cassie is forced by Mr Simms and by Big Ma to apologise to 'Miz Lillian Jean' in front of a crowd. 'No day in all my life had ever been as cruel as this one'(p. 97).

NOTES AND GLOSSARY:
clabber milk: curdled milk
flour-sack-cut dresses: dresses made out of old flour sacks. This is indicative of the poverty and ingenuity of the people
mercantile: an all-purpose store
cuttin' up: making a nuisance of herself

Chapter 6

As they put the wagon away, Stacey tries to explain to Cassie why Big Ma had had to make her apologise. They notice a car in the barn and think it belongs to Harlan Granger. The car is Uncle Hammer's, their father's brother, who has come for a visit. Big Ma, knowing her son's temperament, tries to stop Cassie from telling Hammer about the events of the day in Strawberry. Cassie tells him and he leaves in his car. Mr Morrison prevents him from committing any violence by keeping him up talking all night. Mama explains that Mr Simms believes his daughter to be better than Cassie because she is white. She explains that black people were originally brought from Africa as slaves, like Cassie's great-grandparents' grandparents, and that many white people are still convinced of their own superiority.

The next morning the whole family go to church in Uncle Hammer's car. Uncle Hammer, noticing that Stacey's jacket is too small and rather shabby, gives Stacey his Christmas present early: it is a thick winter coat. At church T.J. teases Stacey about the new coat, saying it makes him look like a preacher. Uncle Hammer takes them all for a drive after church and as they approach the bridge, the Wallaces on the other side, presuming the car is the Grangers', back their car off the bridge to let the Logans cross first. As the Wallace's tip their hats to whom they assume are the passing Grangers, Uncle Hammer touches his hat in reply. As the car speeds past the Wallaces, they realise, with horror, who it is. Mama thinks this was an ill-advised thing to have done.

NOTES AND GLOSSARY:
their German war: Hammer is referring to World War One which lasted from 1914 to 1918. America fought with Britain, France, New Zealand and Australia against the German Kaiser
red-neck: a poor farmer, whose neck is sunburnt from working in the fields. This word has negative associations of ignorance and oafishness
chignon: a hairstyle; a bun coiled at the back of the head
Rebel soldiers: Confederate soldiers who fought for the South
Yankee army: Northern soldiers

| gassed: | allowed an increased amount of petrol and air to pass to the car's cylinders, increasing acceleration |

Chapter 7

Mama discovers that Stacey has given his coat to T.J. Mama's reaction is to make Stacey go and retrieve it but Hammer says that T.J. should keep it, since Stacey has shown himself so easily swayed by other people's opinions. It is nearly Christmas and Papa returns. While Big Ma, Papa and Hammer tell stories, Mr Morrison relates the night his family were killed by night men. The adults talk late into the night, discussing the issue of the Wallace store. If they were to back the shoppers themselves they would put their land in jeopardy.

The children receive books for Christmas. There is a huge meal, attended by the large Avery family. Jeremy Simms comes round to give Stacey a flute that he has made. Papa tells Stacey that a friendship between him and Jeremy would never work out. Stacey puts the flute away in his box of treasured things.

The children are whipped by their father for having visited the Wallace store. Mr Jamison comes to visit. Big Ma signs the land over to her two sons, David (Papa) and Hammer. Mr Jamison offers to back the credit, fully aware that this will make him unpopular with the rest of the white population. They accept his offer. He explains that Harlan Granger will be irritated at their interference, and that the boycott of the Wallace store will also affect him financially. To attempt to seek punishment for the Wallaces as if they had killed a white man will suggest that black and white are equal and this supposition will not please Harlan Granger.

Papa, Hammer and Mr Morrison go to Vicksburg. On their return, Mr Granger pays a visit, threatening to charge his sharecroppers more of their crop, thereby preventing them from paying their debts. Harlan Granger threatens that he will ultimately possess the Logan land.

NOTES AND GLOSSARY:

smoke sausages:	smoked sausages. Smoking is a way of curing and preserving meat
coon:	a raccoon, a greyish brown furry animal with a big paddle tail. It is to be found over much of Northern America and is considered to be vermin, so the fact that the Logans are eating it is a sign of their resourcefulness and shows how they must make use of everything that the land provides
shantytown:	a poor section of a city or town full of ramshackle and makeshift cabins or shacks
free Negroes ... colored folks:	black people recently freed. 'Colored'

was the preferred word for black people at the time in which the novel is set

scairt: scared

sabers: U.S. form of 'sabre', a curved cavalry sword

collateral: Mama is referring to the fact that, because they own their own land, the Logans have something that they can put forward as an assurance that the debts the sharecroppers incur will be paid. However, if the sharecroppers are unable to pay, the Logans will lose their land to pay for the debts. Mr Jamison points out that this could be a very dangerous thing for the Logans to do

The Count of Monte Cristo ... The Three Musketeers: these are both novels by the French dramatist and novelist, Alexandre Dumas (1803–70). His father was a general of the Empire and he was a mulatto; the product of intermarriage between a black and white couple. As Papa points out, Dumas' grandmother was a slave. *The Three Musketeers* (1844) deals with the heroic adventures of D'Artagnan who comes to Paris in the reign of Louis XIII to join the king's musketeers. *The Count of Monte Cristo* (1846) recounts the exploits of another young man on the island of Monte Cristo

Aesop's Fables: Aesop, born in *c.* 570BC, was a Phrygian. He was originally a slave who had received freedom from his master. He chiefly resided at the court of Croesus, king of Lydia, to whom he dedicated the Fables. The Fables tell short stories with clear morals, using animals as characters

Yankee carpetbaggers: carpet bags were travelling bags, originally made from carpet. Carpetbaggers was a derogatory term for those with little or no luggage who were travelling with all they possessed, particularly those who descended on the South, hoping to profit from the Civil War

---

Chapter 8

To the horror of her brothers Cassie starts being friendly to Lillian Jean, carrying her books and calling her Miss. Cassie remembers her conversation with her father on New Year's Day. Papa tells her that situations have to be evaluated and that she has to decide what she wants and is able to fight for. Whatever she does Mr Simms is not to find out. All through

January Cassie is Lillian Jean's slave. At school, their mother fails T.J. again, who has been cheating. T.J. is angry and goes to the Wallace store. That same afternoon Cassie persuades Lillian Jean to go up into the woods. When they are isolated Cassie throws down the books that she has been carrying and beats up Lillian Jean, hitting her only where it will not show. Cassie makes her apologise for the Strawberry incident and for all the names she had called her. Cassie threatens to tell all Lillian Jean's secrets if she tells anyone.

Cassie is in school, and has come first in her examinations. Out of the window she sees Kaleb Wallace, and two other white men, one of whom turns out to be Harlan Granger. She makes an excuse to leave the classroom and sees them entering her mother's room. Her mother is giving a history lesson concentrated on slavery. Mr Granger points out that what she is teaching is not on the syllabus and notices that she has covered up the chart on the inside cover of her books. Mama is fired. The children wait for her after school. Mr Morrison offers to look for work to help the family financially. Papa tells him that he would rather he stayed at the house.

The next day some of the other children at school tell the Logans that they overheard T.J. telling Kaleb Wallace about Mrs Logan's teaching methods. After school the children all go to the Avery house. Stacey leaps on T.J. who denies having said anything. When T.J. returns to school a week later, everyone ignores him. Even though he finally admits and apologises, the Logan children walk away from him. T.J. tells them angrily that he does not need them, that he has better friends who treat him like a man, and, moreover, who are white.

NOTES AND GLOSSARY:

Uncle Tomming: *Uncle Tom's Cabin* was a novel written in 1852 by the white author, Harriet Beecher Stowe. It was a controversial book about the wrongs of slavery, published at a time when America was not willing to face up to them. The Uncle Tom of the title was a strongly Christian slave, and it is to his humility and long-suffering acceptance of his position as a slave that T.J. is referring

prime the gossip pump: Taylor uses the metaphor of a water pump when describing how Cassie coaxes secrets out of Lillian Jean. Pumps need 'priming' with a little water to start them working; Lillian Jean only needs to be addressed as 'Miss'. The metaphor has a second layer of meaning because it hints at the way in which Lillian Jean's secrets are told, that she herself is like a pump

Grinning like a Cheshire cat: the Cheshire cat is a creature in *Alice's Adventures in Wonderland* (1865) by Lewis Carroll (1832–98). At one point its body disappears and all that remains is its grin

Chapter 9

It is Spring and school continues. In contrast to the abundance of the earth, the family stores are running low. Jeremy tells them that T.J. is being friendly with his elder brothers, R.W. and Melvin, and that they do not treat him well. Mr Jamison comes to see Papa. Thurston Wallace has been in town 'talking 'bout how he's not gonna let a few smart colored folks ruin his business' (p. 162). Mama is afraid. Although it is nearly summer Papa does not return to the railroad. He resolves to leave that Sunday. Mr Lanier and T.J.'s father, Mr Avery, come to announce that they have to pull out of the Vicksburg arrangement. Harlan Granger has followed through his threats of demanding an increased share of the cotton and has also told them that if they do not give up shopping in Vicksburg he will put them on the chain gang. They cannot put their families and livelihoods at risk. Mama thinks that Papa should also give up going to Vicksburg but Papa is still resolved and decides to take Stacey too, who is now thirteen. He does not want his son to turn out like T.J., whose parents are unable to discipline him.

Papa, Mr Morrison and Stacey set off for Vicksburg to get the orders of the seven families who are still participating. They leave on a Wednesday morning and are expected back on the Thursday. That evening it rains and a storm begins. It grows later and later and the men do not return. When they finally do arrive, Mr Morrison is carrying Papa. Papa's leg has been broken and his head is bleeding, having been skimmed by a bullet. Stacey explains that on the way home from Vicksburg the wheels of the wagon came off after some boys had tampered with them. As they were mending the wagon a truck containing three men pulled up and one of them shot Papa. Jack, the horse, was frightened and reared up. Stacey was not strong enough to hold him, so the wagon rolled back over Papa's leg. Mr Morrison fought some of the men, injuring them badly. Stacey thinks that they were the Wallaces.

NOTES AND GLOSSARY:

persnickety:	unbearable, pleased with herself
lightning bugs:	like fireflies but bigger. Lightning bugs are about the size of bees. Both fireflies and lightning bugs are insects and the lower part of their bodies are illuminated in the dark
chain gang:	a number of slaves chained together while working

Chapter 10

Papa is up and about. The family do not have enough money but are afraid to let Uncle Hammer know in case he finds out about Papa's injuries. Provisions are low. Two of the Wallace brothers are still laid up. Mr Morrison is out looking for work. Mama thinks he should leave, but Papa wants him to stay. Later Mr Morrison goes to Mr Wiggins's farm and the children all go with him. They are stopped on their way home by Kaleb Wallace. Mr Morrison, with amazing strength, moves the truck out of the way, and they go home.

It is August and hot. T.J. has turned into a thief. Jeremy asks them to come and see his tree house and they refuse. The bank calls in the note. Papa heads off for Strawberry, but Mama prevents him from leaving. They telephone Hammer and he says he will find them the money. On the third Sunday of August the annual church revival takes place. Hammer appears, having sold his car to raise the money. He leaves for Chicago. On the last day of the revival T.J. comes with the Simms brothers, dressed differently and calling R.W. and Melvin by their first names. He is disappointed by his reception in his old community.

NOTES AND GLOSSARY:
ledger: a large book used for recording accounts
The bank called up the note: the bank is refusing to allow the mortgage on their land and insisting that they pay their debts immediately

Chapter 11

It is a hot and humid night and a storm seems imminent. T.J. taps on Stacey's door. He is in terrible trouble. He has been beaten up by R.W. and Melvin after a bungled robbery at the Barnett Mercantile. T.J. had climbed through a window to let the Simms boys in. T.J. had been led to believe they were only taking the gun that he had always wanted and that they would pay for it on Monday. They gave him the gun, but continued stealing. However they were interrupted by the Barnetts. R.W. hit Mr Barnett with the flat of his axe and slapped Mrs Barnett. The Simms brothers beat up T.J. He passed out, and when he came to, he walked the long way home to avoid meeting them again.

Stacey resolves to take T.J. home, and, in the end, the other Logan children accompany them. They walk with him to his house and as they wait for him to get inside they see a convoy of cars arriving. The children watch from the woods as T.J. and his family are dragged from their home, by, amongst others, R.W. and Melvin. The Wallaces accuse him of having robbed the Barnett Mercantile with two other black boys, with whom R.W.

and Melvin claim to have seen him running away from the place. Mr Jamison arrives, and announces that both the Barnetts are alive and that the sheriff will soon arrive to remove T.J. The crowd of angry white men are ready to hang T.J. there and then. There is anger towards Mr Jamison. The sheriff arrives, bringing word from Harlan Granger, who sends the message that he will have no hanging on his land. Kaleb Wallace suggests that they go to the Logan place and 'take care' of Mr Morrison and the children's father too. Stacey sends Cassie to get Papa. Leaving Stacey in the wood, the three children run back to the house. The storm has broken.

NOTES AND GLOSSARY:

Roll of thunder/hear my cry: the book derives its title from the first two lines of this song. It is a blues song about a defiant slave: 'I *ain't*/gonna let him/Turn me 'round' and is particularly appropriate to the view of race put forward by the novel

akimbo: with his elbow turned outwards in an awkward way. This is because Mr Morrison broke it on the way back from Vicksburg

Chapter 12

The children arrive home to find the adults already up. Their father is ready to whip them for being out at night but Cassie tells them everything. Papa takes the gun and goes to get Stacey. The others wait at home, and, smelling smoke, realise that the cotton is on fire. Mama and Big Ma go to fight it with wet sacks, and the children are told to stay at home. The fire is going towards the trees where Papa, Mr Morrison and Stacey are. Jeremy Simms arrives, having seen the fire from his tree house. He tells the children that everyone is fighting the fire, including R.W., Melvin, Harlan Granger and Papa. It starts raining.

The next day Cassie and Little Man go out into the desolate fields. Christopher-John stays at home. T.J. is in Strawberry, and thanks to the fire, any immediate violence has been avoided. Mr Barnett died at four o'clock that morning as a result of his injuries. Cassie realises that her father started the fire intentionally. T.J. may have to go on the chain gang, and Papa tells them gently that he may even have to die. Cassie, who never cries, sheds tears for 'T.J. and the land'.

NOTES AND GLOSSARY:

bolls: the seed vessel of the cotton plant

Part 3

Commentary

The characters

Cassie

Roll of Thunder, Hear My Cry is narrated in the first person by Cassie Logan. The events of the novel are filtered through her perceptions and we often hear her voice directly. For example, after Uncle Hammer grills Stacey about the coat, she says: 'I had no intention of ever facing a tongue-lashing like that. Papa's bottom-warming whippings were quite enough for me, thank you' (p. 118).

Her colloquial tone, with its patterns and phrases of everyday speech, gives us a vivid impression of her character. It also creates a feeling of immediacy because we feel as if we are hearing her speak. The distance between the reader and Cassie as a fictional character is reduced by these feelings of intimacy.

Like all her siblings Cassie is intelligent and confident. She is a tomboy and a loner. No details are given of any school friends and her life is based around her family and her home. She finds her Sunday clothes restrictive and loves to run barefoot. At night she often creeps into her brothers' room. She is successful at school but is often to be found looking out of the window or thinking. Her teacher, Miss Daisy Crocker, describes her as highly strung. We see Cassie's sensitivity when she is subdued after her glimpse of the night men (Chapter 4). She sees them draw up outside the farm, hesitate and then move on. After this experience she is quiet and withdrawn for a week, believing, along with her brothers, that the night men had come to punish them for the hole that they had dug to impede the white children's school bus. However she is also outspoken and at times fierce. Brought up to be aware of her own worth, she is fearless; examples of this are when she hands back her soiled book and when she reminds Mr Barnett of her presence in his shop. More than any other character in the novel, Cassie can be said to develop, partly because it is through her eyes that the events of the plot unfold, and so we are immediate witnesses to her development, and partly because she is used by Taylor to illustrate explicitly the nature of totally unjustified and ingrained racism.

Placed half-way through the novel, when our impressions and esteem for Cassie are established, is the trip to Strawberry, the cruellest day in

Cassie's life. At the market in Strawberry she asks Big Ma why they cannot move to a better position from which to sell their wares: ' "Them's white folks' wagons, Cassie," ' replies her grandmother, 'as if that explained everything' (pp. 89–90). In the Barnett Mercantile she is polite and decisive. She does not understand why she should take second place to a child of her own age; the fact that the child in question is white is not something Cassie even considers as relevant: 'Adults were one thing . . . But some kid who was no bigger than me was something else again. Certainly Mr Barnett had simply forgotten about T.J.'s order' (p. 93).

Unlike T.J. she has not been brought up to consider herself inferior. During the course of time the novel covers she has to realise that some white people consider her to be so. The fact that we are presented with her point of view, and share her view of her own worth, makes the blatant prejudice of white people seem more terrible. Cassie reminds Mr Barnett of their order, and he responds angrily. Cassie, rather than being chastened, is equally enraged: ' "I ain't nobody's little nigger!" I screamed . . . "And you ought not be waiting on everybody 'fore you wait on us" ' (p. 94).

After the incident she tries to understand Mr Barnett's reaction. It is during this moment of thought that she bumps into Lillian Jean, thus initiating her second humiliation of the day. Lillian Jean tells her to apologise, and Cassie does so. Lillian Jean then instructs her to walk in the road, and Cassie refuses to obey this command. Lillian Jean's father, Mr Simms, appears, and forces Cassie off the pavement, making her apologise to his daughter. Cassie is reluctant to do so, and is surprised that Big Ma should make her obey Mr Simms.

The narration also provides Mama's explanation of why Cassie was treated in such a manner, and why the Simms and Big Ma behave in the way that they do. Mama says to Cassie that she has had to grow up a little, explaining to her that in the world outside their home, 'things are not always as we would have them to be' (p. 105). This disparity between the cosy regulated world of the Logan household and the cruel exterior reality, where things 'ain't fair', is forced onto Cassie's consciousness during the course of the novel by the episodes of confrontation that concern her directly, and ultimately by the fate of T.J.

In Chapter 8 Cassie takes her revenge on Lillian Jean, and the way that she does this illustrates her character. Her determination and strength are shown by the way in which she keeps her plan secret and does not succumb to the dismay of her brothers and the taunts of T.J., who are all surprised by the way that she appears to befriend Lillian Jean. She shows her intelligence and understanding of character in devising a plan for revenge that will not involve Mr Simms and that manipulates Lillian Jean's desire for sycophancy. Cassie discovers that she only needs to smile and call her 'Miss Lillian Jean' occasionally in order to hear all her secrets. Every day on the way to school Cassie carries Lillian Jean's books, until one day when she leads her up into the forest. Cassie has had her hair braided especially in order to stop Lillian Jean pulling it, and aims her blows carefully, exacting her revenge for Lillian Jean's behaviour in Strawberry. However, one of the reasons for her secrecy is that her parents, her mother particularly, would never have approved of her violence. The reader too is meant to see the revenge in terms of the moral structure presented by the novel. It is an act which makes Cassie likeable and human, and as such is necessary to the plot. It shows Taylor making her characters flawed and therefore realistic. This results in a more interesting portrayal of racism; it is not as if all black people are presented as perfect, and all white people as evil. The existence of Mr Jamison and Jeremy, Cassie's violence towards Lillian Jean and T.J.'s weak character, all show the author's balanced and convincing standpoint on race.

At the beginning of the novel, Cassie's first impulse is one of violence, a characteristic she shares with her Uncle Hammer. When T.J. relates his behaviour to Claude she resolves that were he to attempt anything similar with her she'd 'knock his block off' (p. 16). In the course of the novel she has to learn to think first and to weigh the consequences of her actions, for example regarding Lillian Jean, and, most difficult of all, she has to learn to acknowledge a point in which personal intervention is impossible, as in the case of T.J.

The novel finishes with Cassie's tears for T.J. and the land. The simple language and appreciation of the land show Cassie as a matured character. Previously Cassie informs us that she seldom ever cried (Chapter 4) and in the first chapter she wonders whether she will ever understand her father's estimation of the land. Together with the reader, she has learned many hard lessons about what her mother bitterly refers to as 'the way of things' (p. 105).

T.J. Avery

T.J. is two years older than Stacey, and, together with his brother Claude, he walks to school with the Logan children. His relationship with the Logan children is not one of friendship, and Cassie finds him especially irritating and unpleasant. He does not have the strength of character that the Logans all possess; his moral weakness finally leads to the firing of their mother. T.J., feeling inferior, taunts the children with his knowledge and patronises them. Nonetheless there is an odd bond of obligation between T.J. and Stacey.

T.J.'s family are poor sharecroppers who work for Harlan Granger. T.J. is thin and stupid, and these two attributes, along with his desire for attention, result in the tragedy that is the culmination of the novel. He is thin enough to get through the window of the Barnett Mercantile, and stupid enough not to realise that he is being used, firstly by the

Simms brothers, and ultimately to satisfy the community at large. R.W. and Melvin Simms befriend him, and having been rejected by his school friends for the part he played in the firing of Mrs Logan he relishes the attention of the older white boys. They get him to climb through the window to let them into the Barnett store, tempting him with the pearl-handled gun that he had always wanted. In his naivity he believes that they will pay for the gun later. Instead R.W. and Melvin begin a full scale robbery which is interrupted by the owners of the store. The Barnetts both receive injuries before the three boys leave. After they have beaten up T.J., R.W. and Melvin, who T.J. considered his best friends, have no scruples in accusing him and 'them two other boys' of having perpetrated the crime.

T.J., for all his cowardliness, bragging and insecurity, is in some ways a tragic figure, particularly in the scene in Chapter 10 when he brings R.W. and Melvin to the church revival, in the hopes of impressing his old friends. T.J. is bewildered by his cold reception, muttering, 'it didn't even make no difference' (p. 193), before setting off for Strawberry. This desire for attention, recognised by the astute Mrs Logan in Chapter 9, is a main constituent of his character throughout the novel. It can be seen in what Cassie refers to as 'his usual sickening way of nursing a tidbit of informa-tion to death' (p. 14) and by the way he patronises the Logan children: 'You see when a fellow's as smart as me, he gets to know things that other folks don't. Now this kind of information ain't for the ears of little kids so I really shouldn't even tell y'all – ' (p. 64).

He is fundamentally a coward. In Chapter 1 T.J. proudly tells the Logans how he made sure that it was his brother, rather than himself, who was beaten for the visits to the Wallace store. He explains to them that other-wise he would have had to take the blame, and even Stacey voices his disgust at this behaviour. T.J. lets Stacey be whipped on account of his cheating (Chapter 4). When Stacey confronts him about having told the Wallaces about his mother's teaching methods, T.J. flounders, lies and tries to blame little Willie. Despite T.J.'s tendency to speak all-knowingly, he is intellectually one of the most restricted and naïve characters in the book. These aspects of his character are exploited and he gets involved in a chain of events bigger than himself. Just as he does not notice Melvin's 'conde-scending smirk' (p. 192) that is all too apparent to Cassie, he does not realise that the Simms boys are laughing at his expense, toying with him, and will ultimately desert him. His words in Chapter 5: 'I'd sell my life for that gun' (p. 92), are ironic when we realise that an inclination to show off may well have cost him his life. The novel ends with T.J. in jail awaiting trial, with a broken jaw and several broken ribs. His sentence could be the chain gang, but it could be death. What is distressing is the fact that T.J. is, in a sense, not responsible for his fate. As Papa says: 'This thing's been coming a long time, baby, and T.J. just happened to be the one foolish enough to trigger it' (p. 207).

Taylor's portrayal of T.J. is unsentimental and honest. He is an unattractive character who grows increasingly unruly as the novel progresses. However, what she also makes clear is that he is not essentially evil but is a stupid victim of an unjust society and, ultimately, we can only feel sorry for him.

Stacey

Like all the children, Stacey is forced by circumstances to grow up quickly. He is three years older than Cassie at the 'manly age of twelve' (p. 112). As Papa points out in Chapter 9, a boy of Stacey's age is 'near a man' who has to know 'man's things' (p. 167). As with Cassie there are particular incidents that can be labelled as formative in Stacey's development. The most important of these is his decision to confess to Mama that he was at the Wallace store (Chapter 4) and the lessons he learns from the coat episode (Chapter 7).

The coat was a Christmas present from Uncle Hammer. T.J. tricks Stacey into giving him the thick wool coat, by telling Stacey that it is too big for him and that it makes him look like a preacher. Hammer insists that Stacey should let T.J. have the coat for good, since Stacey was stupid enough to be affected by T.J.'s teasing. Stacey learns several things from the episode. Firstly he learns that he should never give up something that he wants on account of the intervention of others. This 'lesson' in ownership can be seen in Hammer and Papa's attitude to the land. Possession is all important. Secondly Stacey learns that he must not put the blame on others for his own stupidity and that in future he ought to think for himself. In admitting to Mama that he was at the Wallace store he takes responsibility for his actions, showing himself to be more adult.

His age differentiates him from the others. For example he works with his father in the fields, he is taken to Vicksburg, and he is the only one of the children allowed to fight the fire. Stacey is able to understand the things that Cassie finds difficult to comprehend. In Chapter 6 he tries to explain why she shouldn't blame Big Ma for making her apologise to Lillian Jean. In Chapter 5, although agreeing with Cassie that Barnett was in the wrong for having refused to serve her, and for evicting her from his shop, he adds the qualification: 'I know it and you know it, but he don't know it, and that's where the trouble is' (p. 95). He is aware of the superiority which Barnett, as a white man, automatically feels. Cassie finds this very difficult to understand.

We see Stacey's opinions undergoing change and development in his attitude towards Mr Morrison. He is initially diffident towards him, believing that he is capable of helping Mama on his own. He resents the presence of Mr Morrison: 'Don't need him here. All that work he doing, I could've done it myself' (p. 68). But soon Stacey comes to respect him, particularly after Mr Morrison treats him like an adult when he catches him at the Wallace store. Mr Morrison says that he will not tell Mama that the children had disobeyed her, and that he is giving Stacey the option to tell her himself.

Stacey has a strong moral streak. He gets whipped because of T.J.'s cheating, but his personal code of honour means that he does not incriminate him, even after the event. He does, however, have a tendency to blame himself. He feels responsible for having originated the bus plot. He is the one who organises his siblings into digging a hole in the road in order to incapacitate the white pupils' school bus. Afterwards, when the children believe that the night men are after them because of their action, Stacey feels the full weight of his involvement. He also feels at fault when Papa's leg is broken. Stacey was not strong enough to hold Jack and the wagon wheel rolled over his father's leg.

In Chapter 11 T.J. appears in the boys' bedroom, injured and frightened, having walked from Strawberry after the robbery. Stacey acts upon the obligation that he feels for T.J. and walks him home, accompanied by the other children. Stacey is the only one who stays in the forest and witnesses the entire episode of violence that befalls T.J. and his family.

The fact that Taylor chooses Cassie as narrator, rather than Stacey, is significant as regards her intentions for the novel. Stacey is more moral and serious than Cassie. He is a necessary element in the novel, but his character is not as attractive as the spontaneous and proud Cassie. Moreover, he lacks the innocence which Cassie possesses, and which Taylor uses to illustrate the unfairness of racism.

Christopher-John

Christopher-John is the third Logan child, and is the least prominent of the four children in terms of the plot of the novel. He is sensitive and thoughtful; this is demonstrated when he cries because he wishes Papa could stay with them instead of going back to the railroad, and when he takes Claude away from T.J. in Chapter 1. He is generally friendly and easygoing. The most revealing assessment of his character is in Chapter 1 where, on his way to school, he tries to match the moods of both Cassie and Stacey in order to please them.

This attempt to remain on good terms with everyone and his desire to satisfy the moods and wills of his siblings are part of his character. Yet this aspect of his nature comes into conflict with his dislike of troublesome things since he is aways forced to accompany his brothers and sister. He would rather eat lunch than revenge himself on the bus and he does not want to go to the Wallace store to get T.J.: '"I don't want no whipping!" objected Christopher-John, standing alone at the crossroads. But when he saw that we were not coming back, he puffed to join us, grumbling all the while' (p. 71).

He is equally reluctant about walking T.J. home in Chapter 11, but his fear of being left behind means that he is continually attempting to keep up with his more adventurous siblings. In Chapter 12 however, to the amazement of Cassie and Little Man, he resists their stronger wills and stays at home.

Little Man

The youngest of the Logan children, Little Man, or more properly, Clayton Chester Logan, is distinguished by the importance he gives to cleanliness. He is fanatical about keeping his clothes and possessions free from dirt. He is alert and brittle in the same way that his sister is, and like Cassie, is used by Taylor to enunciate several of the instances of discrimination between black and white. He is the one most outraged by their not having a bus to take them to school, and, because of his obsession with cleanliness, he suffers the most when the white children's school bus sprays them with mud. The others have become used to the situation, whereas it affects him, as indeed it affects the reader, with full force. Equally, it is Little Man who first rejects his school reader, with its offensive chart. He is able to read the columns on the inside page and is insulted by the fact that the black pupils were only given the books when they were eleven years old and in 'Very Poor' condition.

Mama

Although ostensibly narrated by Cassie, in some respects Mama's voice is the voice of the novel, or at least the voice of Taylor. Mama's spoken English, like the prose of the novel, is perfect and relatively free from colloquial Americanisms. Mama is the one to tell Cassie about slavery and to explain white insecurity. She tells her daughter that 'Everybody born on this earth is something and nobody, no matter what color, is better than anybody else' (p. 105). This is the message of the novel. It is Mama's value system that makes the reader feel only reserved approval for Cassie's behaviour to Lillian Jean.

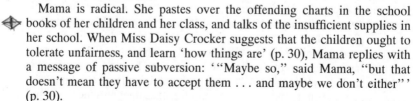

Mama is radical. She pastes over the offending charts in the school books of her children and her class, and talks of the insufficient supplies in her school. When Miss Daisy Crocker suggests that the children ought to tolerate unfairness, and learn 'how things are' (p. 30), Mama replies with a message of passive subversion: ' "Maybe so," said Mama, "but that doesn't mean they have to accept them . . . and maybe we don't either" ' (p. 30).

It is she who organises the boycott against the Wallace store. She goes around the black community, telling people not to shop there, and she enlists the support of other families in their financial resistance. She is pleased about what happened to the bus although the reader senses that she would not have been, had she known the role her children had played. She is firm and strong; we see her splitting her children up when they are giggling, whipping Stacey and standing by her principles when Harlan Granger comes to the school. She is determined and self-aware, knowing that she was fired from her job because she taught what 'some folks just didn't want to hear' (p. 151). Her character verges on being unflawed; she is pretty, brave and charitable and advocates passive resistance. She is not in favour of Hammer's violent methods and, on the night of the T.J. upheaval, she asks Papa not to use his gun.

Papa

Papa is initially a remote figure, working on the railroad. On his return, however, he plays a large part in the main events of the novel. He is injured in Vicksburg and averts the tragedy of Chapter 12 by setting the cotton on fire. He effectively gives a voice to three of the most important themes in the novel. He makes the analogy with the Logan family and the fig tree in Chapter 9. This is one of the few extended metaphors in the novel and can be seen to justify black heritage with the little tree's 'roots that run deep' (p. 166) and its right to belong with the other trees. It is at this point that the idea of personal responsibility is made most clear. In his conversation with Cassie in Chapter 8 he delineates another of the key messages of the novel:

> There are things you can't back down on, things you gotta take a stand on. But it's up to you to decide what them things are. You have to demand respect in this world, ain't nobody just gonna hand it to you. How you carry yourself, what you stand for – that's how you gain respect. But, little one, ain't nobody's respect worth more than your own. (p. 143)

Papa, along with Big Ma, is the person who conveys the importance of the land. Like his brother Hammer he is tough. It is Papa who forbids the friendship between Jeremy and Stacey and stands up to Harlan Granger (Chapter 7). He is more measured and less embittered than his brother however, although Mama accuses him of sounding like Hammer in Chapter 10 after the Vicksburg incident. Papa is a strong disciplinarian and is determined that his 'babies' will not grow up to be like T.J. and whips them for having been to the Wallace store. Even so, he is very proud of his children, and his relationship with them and with his wife is touching. The Logan parents are in perfect harmony, and together they provide the moral structure that informs the novel.

Uncle Hammer

Hammer is Papa's older brother. He works in Chicago, and is, as Harlan Granger describes him, 'right citified'. He is rash and bitter. His violent temper is contrary to the lesson that *Roll of Thunder, Hear My Cry* teaches, that consequences must be weighed. Hammer runs off after Mr Simms when he hears that he has made Cassie apologise to Lillian Jean, and it is only the intervention of Mr Morrison that prevents Hammer from arriving there and endangering himself and the rest of the Logans. He lets the Wallaces think that he is Harlan Granger (Chapter 6) because he and Granger have similar cars. The Wallaces reverse off a bridge to let the Logans pass and tip their hats in respect before they realise their mistake. Mama thinks that they will have to pay for this action. Hammer often talks of burning the Wallace store (Chapter 6, Chapter 7) and of revenge. This aspect of his character works against him sometimes. When Papa's leg is broken the family try to manage without Hammer's help, not wanting him involved. When Mr Jamison approaches them with his offer to back the credit he is sardonic and wary. He is very kind to his brother's family and obviously loves them very much, selling his car on their behalf and buying them generous Christmas presents. However even they experience the hard aspect of his character, particularly Stacey over the episode with the coat (Chapter 7) when Hammer gives him a 'tongue-lashing' (p. 118).

Hammer is significant in terms of the history of the novel. He adds a new dimension to the unfairness. First of all, his presence makes it clear that black people are not treated in the same way across America. He has made money, as can be seen by his car and by the presents that he gives the children. He also mentions twice the fact that black and white fought together in the war: 'You think my brother died and I got my leg half blown off in their German war to have some red-neck knock Cassie round any time it suits him?' (p. 103).

He was injured in World War One, fighting alongside white people, and feels that he has the right to be treated as an equal by them. The reader realises that the racial situation in the South is isolated and that equality is possible and necessary.

Big Ma

Big Ma has a limited role in the events of the novel. She is the oldest representative of the Logan family, the mother of Hammer and Papa, and a matriarchal figure. She helps to establish the domesticity of the Logan home. She is a firm woman, working hard to keep the farm going, and, together with Mama, she is ready to defend the house from the night men. She tells Cassie about her life with Paul Edward and explains to her about the trees. She has to make Cassie apologise in Strawberry, and the reader realises the precarious nature of the Logans' continued safety within the community.

Mr Morrison

Mr Morrison joins the Logan family in Chapter 2, having been brought back by Papa to protect his household. He is described by Cassie as 'the most formidable-looking being' (p. 33) that she and her brothers had ever met. He is enormous, a 'human tree' (p. 33), and his face and neck are scarred. He later explains that his parents were 'breeded stock' (p. 123), slaves mated like farm animals for particular characteristics. His parents were bred for their physical strength. This strength is shown on several occasions; most strikingly, on the return from Vicksburg when he attacks the Wallaces (Chapter 9), and again when he lifts the truck of Kaleb Wallace (Chapter 10).

In Chapter 2 we learn that he was fired from working on the railroad for getting into a fight with some white men and comes to live in a shack on the Logan land. He is not really paid but, in return for his labour and protection, he receives the advantages of home-cooking and a family. During the course of the novel he becomes a less private person. He tells Mama that he would have liked to have had children like her and Papa, and grandchildren like 'these babies of yours' (p. 181). He is the one to stop Stacey and T.J. fighting in the Wallace store and is responsible for preventing Hammer from revenging himself on the Simms. Most importantly Mr Morrison gives the actions of the night men a wider context. We realise the duration of racial violence over the last fifty years, when he tells the harrowing story about Christmas when he was six (Chapter 7). We hear of the almost random violence towards all the inhabitants of his house. Two boys came for respite to his father's house and the white men burst in: 'hacking and killing, burning us out' (p. 122). His sisters die when their home is set on fire, and his parents die fighting.

The moment when he relates this story is one of the few points at which we hear him speak at length or gain any insight into his character. He is presented as a reserved character, and the reader shares the children's awe of him and of the terrible scenes that he witnessed as a child.

Plot and structure

Setting

Roll of Thunder, Hear My Cry discusses the issue of racism. The novel was written in 1976, but it is set in 1933. Racism is still an issue now, but Taylor chooses to place her novel in the past and to give her story of prejudice an historical perspective. There are several possible reasons why she does this. Firstly, she is recovering history. The past in which she places her novel is historically accurate. The South, where conditions had been worsening since Reconstruction, was strongly affected by the Depression. Details of the novel – Papa having to work on the railroad to supplement the family's income, or Mr Avery's pronouncement in Chapter 9 that 'Times too hard' (p. 164) – establish an atmosphere of poverty and hardship.

In the 1930s Mississippi was a focus for racial violence, and the events which Taylor describes – the burning of the Berrys, the tarring and feathering of Sam Tatum and the near-lynching of T.J. – were not uncommon occurrences in the South at that time. Taylor creates an imaginary geography for her novel. The action takes place within a set circumference. There is the Logan farm and the children's school. The nearest town is Strawberry. This is the local market town where Cassie is humiliated, and where T.J.'s crime takes place. There is also Vicksburg, a larger town which is an overnight journey away. Vicksburg is where they shop in an attempt to boycott the Wallace store. In reality, only Vicksburg exists, and it is the one location of which we have no visual impression. There is no Strawberry in Mississippi, although it is a place-name in three other states.

Roll of Thunder, Hear My Cry is a tale of the South. It is precise in general atmosphere but does not tell a 'true story' as such. Taylor plays with this imprecision – her novel does not have to be linked to fact, the events she narrates were happening everywhere. She is remembering no particular family, but all the black families at that time. The racism she presents is commonplace. Cassie and T.J. are made to wait to be served in the Barnett Mercantile. In South Carolina the law insisted that black and white textile workers could not use the same doorways, bathrooms, or even the same water buckets. Cassie resents being told to walk in the street by Lillian Jean, but many cities passed ordinances that kept blacks out of public parks and white residential districts. *Roll of Thunder, Hear My Cry* does not have to be particular to be shocking and it must be remembered that the events in the novel are things that were happening at that time and that continued to happen for many years.

However, there is an autobiographical strand in the novel. Taylor was herself born in Jackson, Mississippi, although she grew up in Ohio. The novel's past is in some respects her past. The story that Big Ma tells in Chapter 4 of the trees was one that was associated with her own family land. The novel is dedicated to Taylor's father who 'lived many adventures of the boy Stacey, and who was in essence the man David'. Taylor weaves her own memories into the narrative.

The novel therefore is a composite of personal experience and historically accurate fiction. By remembering the violence of that time – the night men, the lynching and the fear shared by the black community – and by imparting a sense of that violence and fear to the reader, Taylor is commemorating the past. Moreover, when she wrote the novel in 1976, the Civil Rights movement was beginning to have an effect. *Roll of Thunder, Hear My Cry* is written with confidence of equality. There is a distinctly political aim to the novel. The Logans are shown to deserve equality, in fact to be superior to many of the white families. Taylor is charting a particular stage in the development of black consciousness, when black writers were rejecting the white version of black history. There was felt to be a need to recreate and reclaim stereotypes of black people in literature and in history.

Lastly, Taylor chooses to set the novel in the past because it is more difficult to set racism in contemporary urban life. It is common, especially in children's literature, to use analogies and historical parallels. Defamiliarisation is a common literary technique in order to make the reader consider a situation in a new light. Racism is present nowadays but in 1930s Mississippi it was an acceptable way of life. Characters make no attempt to conceal their blatant discrimination in the novel; for example, the driver of the school bus for white children intentionally accelerates to make the Logan children run into the mud. This type of attitude is accepted, even by some of the black characters. Because racism is presented in such an overt way, only made possible by the distance that history gives, the element of shock is increased.

Purpose

Although in several senses *Roll of Thunder, Hear My Cry* is tied to the politics of its time of writing, the messages it contains are still of great relevance today in the multicultural world in which we live. *Roll of Thunder, Hear My Cry* is a text of educational value. It was specifically written for reading in schools; to recreate the vision of the black world in literature. When asked to comment about her writing for *Contemporary Authors*, a guide to present-day writers in the U.S.A., Taylor made the following statements:

> It is my hope that to the children who read my books, the Logans will provide those heroes missing from the schoolbooks of my childhood. Black men, women and children of whom they can be proud.

She had a specific purpose in writing *Roll of Thunder, Hear My Cry*:

> ... I included the teachings of my own childhood, the values and principles by which I and so many other Black children were reared, for I wanted to show a different kind of Black world from the one so often seen. I wanted to show a family united in love and self-respect, and parents, strong and sensitive, attempting to guide their children success-

fully, without harming their spirits, through the hazardous maze of living in a discriminatory society.

I also wanted to show the Black person as heroic. In my own school days, a class devoted to the history of Black people in the United States always caused me painful embarrassment. This would not have been so if that history had been presented truly, showing the accomplishments of the Black race both in Africa and in this hemisphere. But as it was an indictment of slavery it was also an indictment of the people who were enslaved – a people who, according to the texts, were docile and childlike, accepting their fate without once attempting to free themselves. To me, this lacklustre history of Black people, totally devoid of any heroic or pride-building qualities was as much a condemnation of myself as it was of my ancestors.

Taylor saw a role for her novel. She uses history and the past in a decidedly political way to influence the present and to write the history of the future. As a black writer she is trying to create a new image of black people in literature.

The novel is about racism. It charts Cassie's experience of discrimination and the development of her awareness of black culture. The reader undergoes exactly the same process. *Roll of Thunder, Hear My Cry* is narrated in the first person and this method contributes to its success. Every incident is seen from Cassie's point of view. Time and time again the reader is put in a position in which he or she can share Cassie's understanding of the situation. In Chapter 10 Cassie does not understand why they cannot tell the sheriff and have the Wallaces put in jail, since they know that the Wallaces are responsible for the attack on Papa and Mr Morrison. In this instance, Cassie does not understand why things are not simple. The reader appreciates her feelings. The Logans are presented in such a way that we feel that they deserve to be treated as equals and we appreciate the injustice of their position in society. By showing the Logans as strong and good, and educating the reader at the same time as Cassie is educated, Taylor manages to create a situation in which the reader, of whatever race, learns something of what it felt like to be black in the 1930s. When Mama takes the children to see the burned Mr Berry, to prevent their return to the Wallace store, the reader too is taught a lesson and is horrified by that 'still form' staring at them with 'glittering eyes' (p. 83). Taylor intentionally cultivates this sense of horror and injustice on the part of the reader. She does this to show the unfairness of racism.

Structure

The choice of material in the novel – incidents, characters, stories – and the way these are put together and organised in relation to each other can be called its 'structure'. Examining and analysing this structure will reveal how the effects of the novel are created. For example, it is clear that the most straightforward structural element in *Roll of Thunder, Hear My Cry* is the way in which it builds up to a climax. The novel is almost entirely chronological; in other words, the events of the story happen one after the other. It takes place over a year and there is no shifting backwards or forwards in time. However, the structure of *Roll of Thunder, Hear My Cry* is, nonetheless, most complex. It is highly-wrought and very effective.

The novel relates the growth of racial tension, culminating in T.J.'s misfortunes. The author builds up and varies the degree of the discrimination she depicts. At the beginning of the novel Little Man and Cassie reject the schoolbooks that they have been given. The books were not considered usable by white children. There is a chart in the front cover which shows that the books are eleven years old, that their condition is 'Very Poor' and that at this stage they are worthy to be read by 'nigra' children (p. 26). We learn that the black children do not have a bus to take them to school, whereas the white children do. In Strawberry a shop owner, Mr Barnett, serves Cassie last because she is black. She is thrown out of the shop for complaining about her treatment. Later that same day she is forced to walk in the road and apologise for having bumped into a white girl. These incidents of racism are distressing but are less severe than the premeditated violence of the night men and the extreme cruelty inflicted on the Berrys and on Sam Tatum. These degrees of racism are central to the purpose of the novel. Cassie's life is affected on all levels. However these episodes of racism are alternated with domestic episodes. In Chapter 3 Cassie is awake in the middle of the night. She sees the night men come up to her house and then decide that it is the wrong house. This scene emphasises the fear that is shared by the black community. There is no logic to the attacks of the night men, and nobody is safe. The chapter finishes with Cassie's 'restless sleep' (p. 60). Chapter 4 begins with Cassie churning butter and Big Ma kindling the fire. The provision of this kind of detail means that we see the characters developing and interacting in natural situations. There is a pattern and a purpose to this alternation.

As can be seen from the glosses (see 'Detailed summaries' section, p. 11), the beginning chapters are full of historical detail and Americanisms. The novel is set in the past, and the references help to establish the atmosphere of that time. The reader is given a detailed picture of 1930s Mississippi and becomes familiar with the characters before the plot and the purpose of the novel are allowed to take precedence. This technique can be seen in the first chapter itself. At this point in the novel all that has happened in terms of action is that the children are on their way to school, but in terms of atmosphere and character the reader knows much more. Before we are introduced to T.J., who is the central figure in the novel's main plot or story, and long before we hear of the pearl-handled pistol, the reader learns about the children's lunch of cornbread and oil sausages, of the cotton field, the Depression and the Logan land history. It is, of course, common for stories to set the scene in this way.

The time scale operates in a similar way. The first chapters cover the events of single days in specific detail. The reader comes to 'know' the characters. In contrast Chapters 7 to 10 are episodic, each containing several incidents separate in time and nature. For instance, Chapter 7 includes many different episodes. Stacey admits that he has given T.J. the coat he was given for Christmas. We hear the 'tongue-lashing' that Uncle Hammer gives him. This is followed by Papa's long-awaited return. Then Cassie overhears a conversation about the boycotting. We also learn the details of Christmas morning and witness Jeremy's visit to give the flute to Stacey. The narrative then moves to relate the children's whipping the following day, and Mr Jamison and Mr Granger's visits. Although these episodes deal with the Logans and developments of the plot in a chronological way, the strands are not linked and unified in the same way as they are in Chapter 1. Suspense is being created. We do not know how events will be brought to a conclusion. Chapters 8, 9 and 10 cover a period of about three months. There are several points in which the narrator stands back from the story and comments on things in general. The reader becomes aware of the passing of time, and of the accumulation of tension within the community. This tension is all centred around the Logans. Mama is fired for her unorthodox teaching. Thurston Wallace has been heard to say that he will stop the Logans shopping in Vicksburg. In Chapter 9 Papa is shot on his return from Vicksburg. In the same chapter Kaleb Wallace encounters Mr Morrison and the children on the road. Kaleb threatens Mr Morrison, saying that he ought to shoot him there and then.

The last three chapters return to the detailed style of the first chapters. Chapters 11 and 12 cover the events of the same night. This expansion of detail results in the reader's awareness of the full horror of T.J.'s fate.

Narrative style

The novel is narrated by Cassie. She is the 'I' of the first person narration. However Taylor seems unsure about the extent to which children can realistically be involved in the action she depicts. For this reason many conversations are overheard. This means that the readers are often in a position where they are listening, with Cassie, to her parents' discussions of atrocities, and of the actions which should be taken in reprisal. It is necessary also to distinguish another voice in the narrative. This is the voice of a disinterested observer; an unacknowledged narrator, who can be heard clearly at times (for example at the beginning of Chapter 9). It seems to be the voice of an adult. These sophisticated passages are different in tone from Cassie's frank assessment of situations, but together they give a fuller picture of Logan life.

We are aware of the fact that behind Cassie's account there is her creator, the author. The element of conscious shaping becomes discernible in the instances of 'suspense' and 'hiding' in the narrative. When Cassie befriends Lillian Jean for the purpose of achieving her revenge (Chapter 8), the reader is kept in suspense, not fully aware of Cassie's motives until the final scene in which she takes Lillian Jean into the woods in order to beat her up. The events are not related in a linear fashion. This is the only point in the book where Taylor does not follow a simple temporal sequence. The chapter opens with Cassie running to catch up with Lillian Jean. Then it changes from the present to the past, and relates Cassie's conversation with her Papa. He tells her that she should consider carefully whether or not Lillian Jean is worth taking a stand about, pointing out that she will not be the last white person to treat Cassie in such a way. Cassie promises that Mr Simms will not be involved, and then informs us that she has spent the month of January carrying Lillian Jean's books and calling her 'Miz'. The plan is obviously well formulated, as we discover when Cassie explains that she has had her hair braided in a particular way in order to prevent Lillian Jean from being able to pull it. We are aware that Cassie has been planning some sort of revenge, but her brothers and Lillian Jean are perplexed by her feigned change of heart and are in total ignorance of what is about to take place.

There is another point where Taylor intentionally limits our knowledge in order to create an effect. In the narration our realisation develops in conjunction with Cassie's slow awareness that her father has set the cotton on fire (Chapter 12). We witness Mama pleading with Papa not to use the gun, and see the idea first crossing his mind: 'Papa stared out as a bolt of lightning splintered the night into a dazzling brilliance. The wind was blowing softly, gently towards the east. "Perhaps . . ." he started, then was quiet' (p. 208).

People will assume that the lightning started the fire. The word 'splintered' suggests wood. For a fire to have started, the lightning would have had to strike one of their wooden fence posts. Both Jeremy and Mr Jamison suggest this possibility. The east wind that will spread the fire is mentioned too. On a second reading these hints become more obvious. Papa tells Mama that they both will do what they have to do. He leaves, and soon after Mama smells smoke. Crowding round the doorway the family see the fire billowing, carried eastward by the wind. Big Ma thinks that the lightning is responsible and she and Mama go to fight the fire. Later we hear Mr Jamison telling Papa that he ought to let 'folks' carry on thinking that the fire was an accident. Cassie suddenly understands that Papa had started the fire, that this was the way of preventing T.J. from being hung without using violence.

Language

Several different types of language are often used in novels. There is the language of the characters, or the dialogue, and there is also the language of the main narrator. Most of *Roll of Thunder, Hear My Cry* is written in a straightforward way. This is occasionally lightened by figurative language – the language of metaphors and similes – where comparison is used to give a new aspect to a subject.

The text offers an abundance of natural similes. People and inanimate objects are compared to animals: the bus is 'like a lopsided billygoat' (p. 49), Mr Morrison moves 'like a jungle cat' (p. 59), Stacey 'like a forest fox' (p. 73), and T.J., on the way to Strawberry, chatters 'like a cockatoo' (p. 88), to list only a few. As well as being evocative and apt, these similes also emphasise the presence of nature, and by implication, the land.

A remarkable aspect of the language of the novel is how Taylor makes use of the way in which characters speak. The speech patterns of the characters in *Roll of Thunder, Hear My Cry* are very different from each other. A technique of association is used throughout the story. In her novel, and consequently in the minds of her readers, Taylor associates certain modes of speech with types of characters. For example, the most educated and liberated characters, Mama and Mr Jamison, hardly use the Southern dialect. Moreover, the vernacular used by Big Ma, Mrs Avery and other black characters is distinct from the language of the poor whites. The main difference is the religious element of Big Ma and Mrs Avery's speech, 'Lord have mercy', and their use of the Southern pronoun, 'y'all'. They call their relations 'girl' and 'child', thus emphasising the strength of the community and family relationships. Their speech is soft and rolling. The poor whites also use 'y'all' but their language is harsher. Mr Simms says to Cassie: 'When my gal . . . says for you to get yo'self off the sidewalk, you get, you hear?' (p. 96). He uses 'gal' instead of 'girl'. Generally we see the whites in aggressive situations and so their language is accordingly aggressive. The reader should be aware of this.

It is interesting to note that the speech of Jeremy, his sister and the Wallaces is as ungrammatical as the Averys' or the Berrys' speech. Although they are distinct, the language of the poor black and whites is of the same level. They do not speak like Mama or Mr Jamison. Their poverty and the fact that they have not been educated is shown in their speech, and this shared language undermines the white notion of superiority. Their sense of being better is not endorsed linguistically.

Thus the kind of language that characters use can be seen as an indication of their social status and their role within the hierarchy of educated and non-educated speakers within the novel. There are many different levels of language. Taylor has tried to convey authentic speech patterns by freely using Americanisms and colloquial speech. T.J.'s speech in particular is ungrammatical and he often uses slang: 'I jus' said ole Claude was always sneakin' up there to get some of that free candy . . . I had to go and get him 'cause I knowed good and well she didn't want us up there. Boy, did he get it!' (p. 15).

Taylor wants the reader to be able to imagine what T.J. sounds like. She does everything to make his written words look like they sound, taking off final letters ('jus' . . . sneakin' ') and using colloquial verb forms: 'I knowed'. This is partly for the sake of realism. However, in the larger context of the novel, the way that people speak has great significance. Kinds of language correspond with the characters' true status in the novel. For this reason Mama and Mr Jamison have 'correct speech', or rather a level of speech that matches the prose style of the novel. Mr Jamison reveals his profession as lawyer with his use of balanced clauses and rhetoric when he offers to back the credit (Chapter 7) and Mama quite clearly represents the strong voice of educated and informed morality.

It is relevant to notice that Cassie's speech and thoughts are written in different ways. She speaks in rough dialect but has her thoughts presented in a more standardised English. Sometimes the language of her thoughts is familiarised and becomes very like her speech patterns as, for instance, when she says: 'I had a good mind to go back in and find out what had made Mr Barnett so mad' (p. 95). At other points in the novel Cassie's language is very formal and elevated. Her words acquire great resonance and her situation is magnified. An example of this effect is the last sentence of Chapter 5: 'No day in all my life had ever been as cruel as this one' (p. 97). The most striking example, however, is the last paragraph of Chapter 12. The language is simple and patterned by repeated words and phrases:

> I had never liked T.J., but he had always been there, a part of me, a part of my life, just like the mud and the rain, and I had thought that he always would be. Yet the mud and the rain and the dust would all pass. I knew and understood that. What had happened to T.J. in the night I did not understand, but I knew that it would not pass. And I cried for those things that happened in the night and would not pass. I cried for T.J. For T.J. and the land. (p. 220)

Taylor plays with the difference and overlap between understanding and knowing, and with the contrasting ideas of permanence and change. The euphemism of 'what had happened to T.J. in the night' refers to the violence that the children witnessed from their hiding place in the forest. They see T.J. and his family dragged from their home. His mother is thrown to the ground. His sisters are spat upon and slapped. Claude is kicked and T.J. has his jaw broken. It is acceptable to avoid referring to this violence explicitly because we have shared the horror of the night and still have it in our minds. The formality of the phrase 'would not pass', and its repetition gives the sentences peculiar resonance. Cassie refers to the mud, the rain and the dust, and explicitly mentions the land in the last phrase. The novel finishes with a non-sentence. There is a pattern of 'I' and 'T.J.' or 'he'. Cassie still finds it difficult to understand why T.J. has been selected for discrimination, in the same way that she could not understand why Mr Barnett would not serve her in Strawberry. However, after the course of the novel, she has understood that this injustice will always be part of her life.

Elevated, patterned language of this sort also occurs at other significant moments in the novel, particularly in Papa's analogies and explanations, for example when he compares the Logan family to the fig tree which grows in the yard (Chapter 9) or when he explains to Cassie that she must not only earn respect from other people but that she must respect herself too (Chapter 8). This same style is present in the title and in the beginning of Chapter 9 and also in Cassie's victory over Lillian Jean:

> And she apologized. For herself and for her father. For her brothers and her mother. For Strawberry and Mississippi . . . (p. 147)

Like the novel's final words this passage is not composed of grammatical sentences. They begin with prepositions and often do not have a verb. However they do have a parallel structure. There is a pattern of male and female family members in the order in which Lillian Jean apologises: herself, father, brothers, mother. The shortness of the sentences and the repetition of 'for . . . for . . . for' makes the meaning of the passage seem magnified.

Mr Morrison, when relating the story of the Christmas he passed when he was six, speaks in a similarly elevated style (Chapter 7). He is an elemental figure, due to his huge stature, his incredible strength and his voice like thunder. In his harrowing story he uses biblical language referring to the 'devilish night men' that 'swept down like locusts' (p. 122). The locust plague was one of the plagues that affected the children of Israel in the Old Testament. His parents fought 'them demons out of hell like avenging angels of the Lord' (p. 123). He tends to use very short sentences, a stylistic device described as parataxis. The abrupt effect adds to the horror of the story. Mr Morrison is generally a laconic character and he chooses not to live in the same house as the Logans. His short sentences are indicative of his character.

Characters sometimes use levels of language that are not their own. For example, Harlan Granger persists in speaking in a 'folksy dialect' (Chapter 7) even though he has had a college education. The text implies that this assumed dialect is intentional and associated with Granger's Old South background. Another character whose language fluctuates is Miss Daisy Crocker, Cassie's teacher. She does not understand Cassie and Little Man's wrath at the charts in their books which refer to them as 'nigra'. Cassie appeals to her: ' "S-see what they called us," I said, afraid she had not seen. "That's what you are," she said coldly' (p. 27).

Here is an interesting grammatical point – we have to assume that Miss Crocker is also black, but she chooses to distance herself grammatically from being classed as 'nigra'. Her language when addressing the first grades is patronising and repetitive: 'We shall work, work, work . . . like little Christian boys and girls and share, share, share' (p. 22). Little Man is a member of this class, and, knowing his character and abilities, we can appreciate the inappropriacy of her tone. Mama and Papa do not speak to their children in this way. They explain things to them with the same level of language that they use when speaking to adults. When Miss Crocker is angry she forgets her 'teacher-training-school diction', and lapses into the use of 'ain't' (p. 29). Her language with Mama when they are alone in the classroom is again very different from the way in which Miss Crocker addresses her class.

Themes

Treatment of race

Taylor states that the society she describes is 'discriminatory'. It is interesting that in the first chapter she does not initially say what colour the children are. This is the most significant instance of 'hiding' by the narration. The fact that Jeremy has welts on his arms as a result of associating with the Logan children is inexplicable to the reader, though accepted by Cassie. Only when their school is described is it made explicit that the Logans are black. Of course the reader may well have guessed as much from the novel's opening, particularly if there is a picture on the front cover. However, at the beginning the colour of the protagonists of the novel is not presented as an issue, and yet it will become the main issue of the novel. This technique plays with the reader's attitude to race, making us very conscious of our own racial and cultural assumptions. We are very used to reading novels about white people and might often assume that a book we read will have a white hero or heroine. Taylor, by not referring initially to Cassie's race, forces us to acknowledge this assumption, a form of racism. The fact that Cassie does not use the word black, and that Taylor does not describe the children in terms of colour is because colour-distinctions are made from outside, whether it be by the reader or by society. The words 'nigger' and 'nigra' are words that other people apply to Cassie, and not words that she would use herself.

In Chapter 2, Cassie gives a very specific description of the colour of the characters. Big Ma has smooth skin that is the colour of a pecan shell, whereas Mama is 'tawny-coloured' (p. 32), and Mr Morrison's skin is of 'the deepest ebony' (p. 34). These variations are all subsumed by the word 'black'. Cassie gives these details as a way of creating a visual picture of Big Ma, Mama and Mr Morrison. They are presented along with details of height and shape as physical characteristics, in order to help us imagine the characters. They are not used as a racial indicator.

Taylor chooses to convey racism in a very subtle way. The text presents the historical events of 1930s Southern America to an audience ignorant of their nature. Taylor presents the novel from the point of view of a nine-year-old girl, whose family is independent enough to have preserved her in ignorance of the world outside. In doing so, Taylor creates a character whose situation is like that of the reader. Cassie and the reader develop together and are exposed to the same experiences. Taylor can be seen as a didactic writer. She has a particular set of lessons that she wants to teach her readers, and she uses the character of Cassie to impart these lessons.

Taylor chooses to deal with the effects of prejudice, rather than the motives for prejudiced behaviour. This is conveyed to the reader very clearly by the way in which the narrative is structured. The author does not analyse in depth the motives of her white characters. We see their nastiness, selfishness and greed and their inability to see black people as human beings. We witness their actions but are never allowed into their characters to see their motivation. We see the effect of these actions on the black community. This makes it very difficult for the reader not to sympathise entirely with the Logans, which, of course, is exactly the effect that Taylor intends.

Jeremy Simms has an interesting role, in so far as his character shows that racism affects white people too. He and Stacey can never be friends until the system changes, until black people have equality with white people. In Chapter 7, Papa tells Stacey that his friendship with Jeremy is doomed. Although for the moment they might be friends, in a few years the differences between them would become apparent and Jeremy would 'turn' on Stacey. Stacey does not think that this would be the case, but has to agree with his father that the costs of attempting such a friendship are too high. Thus Jeremy's character provides balance and contrast in the structure of the novel. Mr Jamison is another character who regards black people as equals. Cassie remembers him as the only white man she had ever heard addressing Mama and Big Ma as 'Missus' (Chapter 6). By presenting unprejudiced white characters, Taylor complicates the novel and makes it more realistic. No race should be generalised, and Taylor does not present all black characters as good, or all white characters as bad. T.J. is the 'bad' black person. Although he is not intrinsically evil he is weak, as is shown throughout the novel. He is presented as a cheat, a liar and a coward, and is led astray by white boys. T.J. is balanced by Jeremy, the 'good' white. Of course, neither one of these characters is completely good or bad, but they do provide contrast and balance to the novel and increase the element of realism.

There are parallels between the upbringings of Granger and Jamison, and of Jeremy and his siblings. The fact that Jeremy has managed to be different from his father and from Lillian Jean, R.W. and Melvin, provides some hope for the racial situation. It is worthwhile to notice how young Jeremy seems when, for example, he comes to the Logan farm on the night that the cotton is on fire. He has been sleeping in his tree house, and is completely ignorant of what has passed that night. He does not seem to know about T.J.'s crime or about the role his brothers have played. He is not aware of the unlikelihood of Stacey and his being friends. Although he is continually rejected by the Logans, he continues to attempt to be friends with Stacey, making him a flute for a Christmas present, and inviting all the children to visit his tree house. He is like Cassie in his ignorance and innocence, but, instead of growing up in the way that she has to, he does not have to come to terms with anything. He does not develop as a character. Taylor does not allow Stacey and Jeremy to become friends within the context of her book. This would be sentimental. The issues that divide black and white at that time reach beyond people's attempts to make friends, and to resolve the problems posited by the novel by making Jeremy and Stacey such a blatant emblem of hope would be too easy a conclusion.

Black heritage

From what Taylor herself says, we know that she wanted to give a positive version of black history, showing black people as proud and heroic. Her novel does present a strong sense of black heritage. History plays an important role. In the author's note at the beginning of the novel Taylor writes:

> From my father the storyteller I learned to respect the past, to respect my own heritage and myself.

When Papa is talking to Cassie about how and whether she should seek revenge on Lillian Jean (Chapter 8), he tells her that she must earn respect and, above all, that she must respect herself. This is what Taylor learned from her own father, and what she hopes to teach her reader.

In *Roll of Thunder, Hear My Cry* Taylor chooses the past as a setting. She sees herself as recovering the history of black people, a history which she believed had been misrepresented in white literature. The novel is interspersed with many references to slave history. Mama is teaching about slavery on the day that she is fired. She is explaining its cruelty and the way in which the states profited from 'the free labor of a people still not free' (p. 149). It is typical of Taylor's method that the reader too should hear the substance of Mama's lesson, and learn apace with her pupils. The reader encounters the concept of slavery on many levels. We hear of Papa

Luke, Cassie's great grandfather who was a slave and who ran away before being caught and punished, and of Mr Morrison and his parents. When Mama is explaining Mr Simms's motivation in behaving as he does to Cassie, she explains the history of the Civil War and of slavery. The essential insecurity that prompts white prejudice is gently related:

> So now, even though seventy years have passed since slavery, most white people still think of us as they did then – that we're not as good as they are – and people like Mr Simms hold on to that belief harder than some other folks because they have little else to hold on to. (p. 107)

One of the ways in which rhetoric can be used is to be unobtrusive. This is very different from strident and noisy rhetoric but at times can be just as forceful. Mama is a teacher, who succeeds in teaching her daughter without Cassie realising that she is being taught. At the same time, Taylor, also a teacher, is quietly teaching the reader.

The children are made aware of the land and of its history. Cassie is almost able to recite the way in which her grandfather procured their acres. The oral nature of their community is stressed. The author's note alerts the reader to the importance of story-telling. Historically, telling stories was important to black literature because it was the main mode of recording what Taylor refers to as 'a history not then written in books'. In *Roll of Thunder, Hear My Cry* there are many instances of oral narratives, whether it be Big Ma telling stories of the trees and of her husband in Chapter 4, or the night of Papa's return in Chapter 7 when Papa, Uncle Hammer, Big Ma, Mr Morrison and Mama 'lent us their memories, acting out their tales with stageworthy skills' (p. 121), and imitating the characters they depict so well that the children hold their sides with laughter. We hear Mr Morrison's story of the massacre of his family. Papa tells Mama: 'These are things they need to hear, baby. It's their history' (p. 122). The power of recollection keeps the past alive. The characters are shown remembering, just as the novel remembers and commemorates black history, giving an affirmation of black culture and heritage.

Education

A subject which recurs throughout *Roll of Thunder, Hear My Cry* is education. The novel is preoccupied with school, books and language use. Education equals power in the novel. T.J. is intellectually and morally weak. We see this early on from his cheating and his failure at school. When Little Man is upset about the way in which the bus daily dirties him, Big Ma consoles him by telling him to ignore 'them ignorant white folks' (p. 42). She assures him that one day he will have plenty of clothes and perhaps even a car of his own, provided that he studies and gets himself an education. Here education is linked with money and power.

However, education can be used in a negative way. Mama tells Cassie about the way in which Christianity was manipulated in order to teach black slaves to be loyal and to accept their condition. The power of received knowledge is strong and can be misapplied. Education can be used to keep sections of a community in a disadvantaged social state.

Taylor objected to the school books of her childhood. She did not feel her history had been presented accurately. In *Roll of Thunder, Hear My Cry*, she is trying to create a new version of what it means to be black in school literature. Her novel for children is written with an explicit didactic purpose. The reader senses the inappropriacy of the school textbooks in her novel. They portray girls with 'blond braids' and boys with 'blue eyes' (p. 23). This has no relevance to the community that Taylor is showing us, the ill-equipped school and poorly-dressed dusty children with which we are familiar. The only other books that the children possess are the ones that they receive for Christmas in Chapter 7. There is a sharp contrast between the two sets of books. The school books are inappropriate and unwelcome. The Christmas books are welcome and appropriate. The difference is best illustrated by Little Man's reactions. He initially rejects the books he is given at school, firstly for their condition, and secondly, because of the chart printed on their inside cover. He is overjoyed to receive his book at Christmas, and its pristine condition means that he covers it and washes his hands continually in order to avoid soiling it. The books the elder two children receive for Christmas are also presented in terms of a visual image, this time though the image is more relevant than that of the rich white girls in their textbooks. The Christmas books are written by Alexandre Dumas, whom Papa informs them was a black man. There is a picture of him in 'a long, fancy coat' (p. 127). Papa explains that Dumas's father was a mulatto and that his grandmother had been a slave.

Depiction of women

Women are shown to hold great strength in the Logan family. Big Ma owns the farm, and she and Mama run it, with the help of the children and, under normal conditions, only occasional visits from Papa and Hammer. There is equality between the sexes. In conversation Mama and Cassie are as vocal and contribute as much as either Papa or the boys. Mama is the most educated figure in the novel, and Cassie is given the same schooling as her brothers.

The domestic chores are shared between the women and children. The women, however, are solely responsible for the cooking, and Cassie is often shown helping Mama and Big Ma. We hear of the preparation of food and witness the appreciation of the men: 'These womenfolks done gone and fixed us a feast' (p. 162). The narrative is also appreciative. There are lavish descriptions of food. Cooking and ingredients are lovingly described, whether it is the making of butter, cornbread, or beans. Meals are an important social occasion and their preparation is described as a skill.

Moreover, the women show themselves capable of many other activities, thus attaining almost heroic stature. Other than cooking, there is no distinction between 'female' and 'male' work. Big Ma and Mama fight the fire, work in the fields and guard the house with guns. Cassie is a tomboy, and Little Man is more concerned for his clothes than she is. Taylor does not present any stereotyped view of the way that girls and boys should be. The issue of inequality is reserved for the racial sphere. The reader's attention is focused on the one dominant instance of injustice. Nothing detracts from the main theme of racism.

Sense of community

There are two accounts of feasts. One is on Christmas day and the other is at the Revival. Both are remarkable for their evocative listing of food. This, combined with the detail of home and family life, gives the reader a deep impression of the strength of the black community. In contrast, there is no equivalent portrayal of the white community. We do not see the white families cooking and eating together. Instead we hear only of Jeremy's tree house and witness the intolerant and aggressive behaviour of white adults in public. At times they show their ignorance, or are menacing, for example, Harlan Granger coming to quietly threaten, the night men in their cars outside the Logan farm, or Mr Barnett's violent behaviour to Cassie in the mercantile. We see the closeness of the black community; the prevailing sense of social responsibility is shown by Big Ma's visiting the Berrys with her medicines and Mama taking food to the Berrys. Mama organises the boycott and warns parents of the dangers of the Wallace store. The black families are given character and humour whereas the white are limited. Indeed we only learn about the existence of the white families during racist episodes. We never see the Simms's home-life, or witness comparable family scenes.

However, the Simms are the only other family of which we have any impression at all. We see Mr Simms's angry gaze at Jeremy when his son stands up for Cassie. Jeremy senses the richness of the black sense of community and longs to become part of it. There is the sad scene in which he is excluded from the Logans' Christmas celebrations. Stacey puts the flute that Jeremy gives him into his box of treasured things but he does not play it even once. It is valued, but not for what it is. It is a sign of hope but is regarded as futile in the social situation that prevails. Jeremy is lonely and excluded from the white community, shown by his wanting to live in a tree house, from which he pretends that he can see the Logan farm.

He surprises Stacey by saying that he doesn't really like his siblings. Stacey replies that: 'A fellow's gotta like his own kin' (p. 159). The white families are presented as having a diminished sense of community.

The novel is far from merely glorifying black culture. This would be too simple. The black community is not presented as perfect, as can clearly be seen by the whole nature of T.J.'s character and his behaviour. This is the most striking and central example of the way in which Taylor develops her main characters, making them fallible and therefore likeable. There are two incidents of revenge: when the children dig a hole to stop the bus and when Cassie beats up Lillian Jean for having made her apologise to her in Strawberry. Though amusing, neither of these episodes are particularly edifying. In terms of the moral structure of the book we are not meant to think them so. There are reasons why both incidents are kept a secret. The reader feels that Mama would not approve of either of these episodes.

The hole in the road could have caused an accident. After they have immobilised the bus, the children are frightened by what they have done because of the appearance of the night men. However, even before the evening is over they are sobered by the thought that Mama might have fallen into the hole.

Cassie is vicious in her behaviour towards Lillian Jean. This is behaviour that Hammer advocates and not behaviour which the book supports. Cassie shows no mercy for Lillian Jean and effectively punishes her for the wrongs of society. Cassie makes her apologise for Mississippi itself. Lillian Jean has been brought up to think herself superior, and, in a sense, her behaviour is not only her fault, but the fault of her parents and of society as a whole. However the degree to which Lillian Jean absorbs and accepts her superiority ensures that she is not a character who obtains our sympathy. Cassie's anger is against all the racism she has experienced, but is directed only at Lillian Jean, the example of it within her reach. We may sympathise almost wholly, but we cannot condone her violence. However, Taylor gives us every reason for sympathy, for example, by stating that Cassie is younger than Lillian Jean, thus making sure that her behaviour cannot be confused with bullying.

Both the nature of racism and the strength of black culture are presented in a complex way in the novel. It shows poor whites needing to feel themselves superior to the poor blacks because they have little else. At the same time, Taylor makes it clear that this feeling of superiority is completely unjustified. Perhaps the most brilliant illustration of this unthinking assumption of superiority is the disturbing ease with which Lillian Jean accepts Cassie's change of heart. Her reaction when Cassie offers herself as a penitent slave is the self-satisfied: 'Well, I'm glad you finally learned the way of things . . . God'll bless you for it' (p. 140). She is incapable of realising that Cassie's friendliness had all been a game, shouting after her: 'But, Cassie, why? You was such a nice little girl . . .' (p. 148).

The Logan children, isolated by their independent status, have grown up unaware of the prejudice that their race will incur. Cassie cannot believe that it is because of Lillian Jean's colour that her father believes her to be superior. 'Ah, shoot! White ain't nothing!' she says, incredulously (p. 105). In this way the Logans illustrate and effect Taylor's intentions for her novel. They are as confident as she is in their portrayal. They can be seen in contrast to T.J., who is so proud to think he has white friends and who does not resent his treatment in the Barnett Mercantile. He either accepts his treatment as an inferior or is deluded into thinking himself an equal. The Logans fight discrimination in their own ways. This fight against injustice is the subject of the novel, and the *Roll of Thunder, Hear My Cry* itself is part of the fight against discrimination in the world at large.

The land

The land is described so many times that it can almost be considered as a theme in the novel. We are constantly reminded of its physical existence as earth, dust and mud. Given that the novel is set in a farming community it is not surprising that the land's produce features strongly in the narrative. Cotton rules the school term dates which are structured around the times at which the black children have to help their parents in the fields. The reader witnesses the Logans' symbiotic relationship with the land, the work they put in in return for their independence. In Chapter 1, Papa predicts that Cassie will understand the central significance of the land, and on the final page of the book she cries 'for . . . the land'. These are the last words of the novel, and, at that stage, 'the land' has obtained a far-reaching and many-faceted meaning for Cassie and for the reader.

Firstly, the land has the power to impede. The dust and the mud that the children encounter on their way to school is conveyed vividly. At times the land is actually personified, for example at the very beginning of Chapter 3, when the rain falls on dust which 'had had its own way for more than two months' (p. 40). Secondly, the land is a possession that represents the Logans' independence. In an indirect way, it stands for the unity of their family. Papa tries to explain it to Cassie in Chapter 1:

> All that belongs to you. You ain't never had to live on nobody's place but your own and long as I live and the family survives, you'll never have to. That's important. (p. 12)

Cassie does not understand how the land can belong only to her, thinking that it is divided between all of the Logans. She comes to realise that the land stands for something much larger. Although Cassie may not think she understands the importance of the land, she shows herself fully aware, aged only nine, of all the ins and outs of the mortgages and debts. The force of ownership to which Papa refers so early on in the novel is of great relevance. The fact that they own their own land is what differentiates the Logans from all the other families. For black people dispossessed of their country and their culture, this independent status and the sense of their right to be there, like the fig tree in the yard, is very important. Harlan Granger wants to possess their land. This desire is symbolic of the old South's attempts to prevent black people attaining equality. His attempts on the land translate directly as attacks on the Logans' independence.

Three kinds of terrain are presented – the cotton fields, the forest and the road. All three play an active role in the plot in so far as they are crucial sites for incidents in the plot. There are the cotton fields, the Logans' livelihood, where they all work and from which they see Papa returning from the railroad with Mr Morrison. When Papa sets the cotton on fire the fields are what save T.J. from being lynched. It is the protection of the fields that re-unites all the community. Cotton is something that they all have in common. Even the Wallaces who do not farm make their living from trade with farmers.

There are also the trees. These come to symbolise white threats and evil. In Chapter 8 Papa warns Cassie that Mr Simms should not discover her revenge on Lillian Jean. If he did, then Papa would have to get involved and then there would be trouble: 'B-big trouble?' she says: 'Like the trees?' (p. 144). Big Ma explains the history of the trees to Cassie in Chapter 4. They were cut in the summer after Mr Andersen came from Strawberry with an offer to buy them. The offer was backed by a threat, and Big Ma was afraid. Andersen's lumbermen came and chopped down all the trees. Although Papa intervened, many had already been felled, and still lay rotting in the clearing. The trees were important to Cassie's grandfather, Paul Edward. He and Big Ma used to go up there and sit together. The trees, therefore, can be seen to show the violation and desecration of memory, of the white invasion of black culture. The trees themselves are personified in Chapter 8: 'our fallen friends', 'sentinels' and 'the soft mourning of the forest' (p. 142) pre-empts the mourning for humans that is to end the novel. The trees are part of the forest from which the Logan children witness the violence committed upon T.J. and his family, and are also the site of Lillian Jean's apology.

The road is the final type of land. On the way to school it embodies some of their hardships. Their conflicts with the bus are the novel's first attempts to convey racism. The children's battle with the various kinds of weather reminds the reader of the kind of community which is being portrayed. The long walk to school, accompanied by these difficult conditions, almost represents the difficulty of obtaining an education. Cassie speaks of the three and a half hour walk other children have before they get to school. The road provides a link throughout the novel, and is present in both the opening and closing pages. Its use reminds the reader that it is a child's perspective because so much of the plot occurs on the children's way to and from school. The road is the scene of the menace of the bus and the children's solution. It is where we become familiar with the character of T.J. and where Cassie establishes her false relationship with Lillian Jean. This use of the road gives cohesion to the narrative.

Symbolism

Roll of Thunder, Hear My Cry is a novel in which constant references to seasonal change amount to a kind of pattern. The reader is always aware of the weather. The events take place during the course of a year, beginning on an 'August-like' (p. 9) October morning and ending with the thought of how Cassie will feel 'Come October' (p. 219). The reader is aware of the growth of the cotton, of the weather and of the road on the way to school. They struggle with the weather on their way to school in the same way that they battle against the bus. The seasons are sometimes spoken of generally: 'Spring. It seeped unseen into the waiting red earth' (p. 158) where the earth is given the human characteristic of waiting.

Continuity is conveyed by the patterns of crop growth and harvest, and by the change of the seasons. Several passages in the novel play on this idea of predictable, regulated mutability, or change. When Little Man is dispirited by his constant dirtying by the bus Big Ma says: 'Lord, child, don't you know one day the sun'll shine again' (p. 42), and in the final pages of the novel Cassie acknowledges the changing of the seasons as a metaphor for impermanence. Although she understands that 'the mud and the rain and the dust would all pass' (p. 220) she does not understand what has happened to T.J., comprehending, though, that it will not pass.

At times, weather echoes the events of the plot. This may be referred to as 'the pathetic fallacy', where a character's feelings and a novel's atmosphere correspond exactly with the weather. This technique is also common in films. There are storms during moments of fear and excitement. The reader is so aware of the seasons and of the weather in the normal course of the novel, that this relationship between the weather and periods of emotional intensity seems natural and is effective. There is a storm in Chapter 9, when Papa, Stacey and Mr Morrison are on the way home from Vicksburg. The rain and thunder prevent them from hearing the approach of the night men. The detail of the thunder rumbling, and, in the aftermath of the crisis, of the rain softly falling on the roof, does nothing but intensify the drama of the events of the plot. There is also a storm on the night that Mr Avery comes to warn Mama of the presence of the night men (Chapter 3). His visit takes place after the bus incident, and the children do not hear his explanation because of a clap of thunder.

In many works of literature storms are used as an effective metaphor for a violent release of energy after tension. One of the main tensions created by this novel is the feeling that the Logan family is marked out for victimisation. The reader is aware that they in particular are a threat to white supremacy, and we fear that they may have overreached themselves. However the family manages to escape the worst atrocities due to their skill and cunning. The person who does bear the brunt of the growing vexation in the white community, however, is the hapless T.J. The final storm is the most impressive one in the novel. The weather is as violent as the corresponding human events and provides the climax to which everything has been heading. The heat beforehand is oppressive: 'The heat swooped low over the land clinging like an invisible shroud . . . the drying cotton and corn stretched tiredly skyward awaiting the coolness of a rain' (p. 181).

The heat is described using active verbs, as something capable of swooping and clinging. This has associations of a bird of prey, or perhaps a scavenging animal. A shroud is the piece of material used to cover a dead body, and so, with this simile, the heat is given both physical presence and negative connotations. The crops are also personified, portrayed as waiting for the rain to come. This feeling of waiting and of suspense is the same feeling that informs the community and the reader. The novel awaits the outcome of the growing racial tension. In Chapter 12 the Logan children, hearing that Stacey and Papa are safe, celebrate the falling of rain, which echoes their relief and release.

On the night of T.J.'s crime there is no wind and it is unbearably humid. After witnessing the storm of hatred at the Avery place the storm itself approaches: 'The thunder was creeping closer now, rolling angrily over the forest depths' (p. 200). The storm, which is both metaphorical and meteorological, finally breaks in the last paragraphs of Chapter 11: 'Thunder crashed against the corners of the world and lightning split the sky . . . but we did not stop. We dared not. We had to reach Papa' (p. 205). The storm is described in all-encompassing terms. It seems that the whole world is being rocked. The short sentences convey the urgency of the moment. They have sensed the approach of the storm in the same way that Mama predicted that T.J. was 'headed for a whole lot of trouble' (p. 168). Amongst the white people too there is a desire for release and for the violent catharsis of a storm.

The novel finishes with Cassie's tears, as she cries 'for . . . the land'. There is a correspondence between these tears and the final rain that refreshes the crops. The rain represents a long-awaited change in season. Cassie's tears mark a change in her character and outlook that is anticipated by the reader.

Part 4

Hints for study

In order to be ready to write an essay on a text you must know the text in question extremely well. For this reason you should read *Roll of Thunder, Hear My Cry* as many times as possible. A good habit when reading is to make notes on characters and on any scenes that strike you as particularly relevant. Familiarise yourself with scenes and characters so that you can refer to them in detail. Think about each of the characters and how they change in the course of the novel. Try to identify the scenes which show this development. It is valuable to memorise a few phrases that describe characters perfectly and that will be useful in many different essays.

Were you asked to write about Stacey's development as a character you should note the contrast between the way in which the reader sees him in the first chapter, when he is presented as a child who does not want to be taught by his mother, and the way that we feel towards him in the last chapter when he has to accept that his friend may have to die. We witness Stacey developing. A memorable moment in this development is the scene in which Uncle Hammer reproaches him for having been tricked into giving away the coat he was given at Christmas. We remember Uncle Hammer's stern reprimand, and also the word that Cassie uses to describe it: 'tongue-lashing' (p. 118). Of all the children, Stacey, the eldest, is the most aware of the racism that surrounds them. Before the first visit of the night men he asks his mother if he can help her, and through the course of the novel, we see him being allowed to take more and more responsibility as he grows increasingly involved in adult life. Papa takes Stacey with him to Vicksburg and they get attacked on the way home. The reason his father takes him to Vicksburg is to prevent him from turning out like T.J. It is impossible to make comparisons between the two boys; Stacey has a strong moral streak, whereas T.J. is a cheat at school and a coward, letting his younger brother take the blame for his misdemeanours. Stacey gets blamed for T.J.'s cheating, and is whipped by his mother in front of all his classmates. Stacey is quite a serious character, and he remains so throughout the novel.

Though there is a strong sense of overall plot the novel can be broken down into separate episodes. It would be useful to group these episodes into types of events, for example identifying domestic events that establish the Logan family atmosphere, or assembling all the racist episodes that shock and teach the reader. You should think about the relation of these episodes to each other, and about the way in which the book is written. There is an intrinsic pattern to each chapter. Think about the weather, the time-scale and the proportion of general and particular passages. It is important to be sure that you understand the financial aspect of the novel and that you comprehend the basic historical references to the Civil War. Remember when you are reading that every scene and word has been used to create an effect. Think hard about what that effect is, and why the author is seeking to create it.

On one level, the novel can be seen as a carefully designed structure to obtain sympathy for Cassie and for the black cause. Cassie herself, a young child, has to learn what being black means, and the reader goes through the same process of learning that she does. It is worthwhile to consider how Taylor succeeds in establishing sympathy between the reader and her main character and the narrator of the story. What makes Cassie likeable? How does the episode of revenge on Lillian Jean affect our feelings towards Cassie? She is presented as a realistic character, with her bad temper and quick tongue.

Essay titles are only set if there is plenty to say about them. Moreover, the titles often cover the same broad areas. If you have prepared carefully, your knowledge of the text can be applied to any question. When writing an essay, either for assessment or in an exam, choose your title carefully, and, straight away, jot down all the scenes and ideas that you see as relevant to it. Organise these rough notes into some kind of order before you start writing. If possible, try to start your essay in an interesting way, perhaps with a quotation in order to catch the attention of the examiner. You can disagree with any generalisations that the title makes, and if the title uses a quotation you should say at what point in the novel it occurs. Your first paragraph should be quite general, and your last paragraph should provide a conclusion of sorts. Essays do not have to be long, but they do have to be clear and reasoned.

Specimen questions

Here are a number of possible questions on the text, treating aspects of characterisation, themes, narrative technique and language. Specimen answers are provided for three of them:

(1) Does the description of the seasons and of the weather enhance the action of Roll of Thunder, Hear My Cry, and if so, in what ways?

(2) To what degree does the writer make it possible to sympathise with T.J. Avery?

(3) Illustrate the importance of the land, including all the possible interpretations of the concept.

(4) 'I also wanted to show the Black person as heroic' (Mildred D. Taylor). Do you think she succeeds in this aim?

(5) Connect at least three incidents from the action of the book to the specific moral messages that Cassie learns from her family.
(6) Is *Roll of Thunder, Hear My Cry* simply a novel about growing up?
(7) Who do you think is the intended audience of *Roll of Thunder, Hear My Cry*, and why?
(8) Explore the different kinds of language used in *Roll of Thunder, Hear My Cry*.
(9) Describe the relationship between Cassie and Lillian Jean and give your reaction to Cassie's solution.
(10) Discuss the motif of the pearl-handled pistol in the moral pattern of the book as a whole.

Specimen essays

(2) To what degree does the writer make it possible to sympathise with T.J. Avery?

Although Taylor makes it very difficult for us to like T.J., we can still sympathise with him to a certain degree. As a character in *Roll of Thunder, Hear My Cry* T.J. has parallel importance to Cassie, the narrator of the novel. However, as he is presented through Cassie's eyes, the reader is not allowed to make an independent judgment of him. Therefore the degree to which we are allowed to sympathise with T.J. is very much governed by how Cassie relates to him through various incidents in the book.

We are introduced to T.J. in the first chapter of the novel, and, like Cassie, we are disgusted that he has behaved as a coward. He blames his visit to the Wallace store on his brother Claude, who then gets beaten by their mother instead of T.J. Later he cheats in his exam at school and passes his notes to Stacey. Stacey, on being caught with the notes, is whipped by his mother in front of all his class-mates and is failed in the exam. T.J. does not own up and, after school, runs away to the Wallace store in the hope that Stacey will not follow him there. When Stacey does meet him and they fight, T.J. is the one who tells the Wallaces about Mama's teaching methods and is therefore instrumental in her being fired. Afterwards he lies about what he has done and tries to blame Little Willy.

Such incidents do not inspire much sympathy in the reader, and we can only see T.J. as flawed and weak, without any redeeming qualities. Cassie does not like him, and the reader is shown exactly why she feels this way. T.J.'s manner, for instance his irritating way of 'nursing a tidbit of information to death', is as annoying for the reader as it is for Cassie.

However, despite the depiction of T.J. as an unattractive character, the reader does still have a degree of pity for him. Taylor has included seve poignant scenes which encourage this view. When he finally returr school after the firing of Mrs Logan all the children ignore him. H up to Christopher-John and Little Man saying that at least they are still his friends, but they too shun him, even placid Christopher-John. When he finally admits that he is responsible for Mama losing her job, the Logan children walk away from him. He is likewise rejected when he comes to the annual Revival. On the night of the robbery at the mercantile, T.J. takes R.W. and Melvin to the gathering at the black church, hoping to impress everyone. He is dressed in a jacket and unpatched trousers and calls R.W. and Melvin by their first names. R.W. and Melvin are only accompanying him so that afterwards he will come with them both to Strawberry. Instead of the intended effect, the Logans and the other children behave coldly towards T.J., and he is left alone and puzzled. Even Cassie feels sorry for him. This is a memorable scene, and even Cassie is moved by his plight. We are shown his weaknesses, but feel that had everyone behaved differently towards him, he might not have gone to the mercantile.

This is a clever ploy by the author as the feelings of pity build up over such incidents and encourage the reader to feel genuine sympathy for T.J. in the last scene. We witness, along with the Logan children crouching in the forest, an appalling scene of racial violence. T.J.'s parents are thrown to the ground, his sisters are spat upon and he himself is beaten up for the second time that evening. All the other episodes of racial violence in the novel, for instance the incident with the Berrys, and Mr Morrison's past, are narrated second hand and therefore do not have the same vivid quality as the events of Chapter 11. The fact that we do not like T.J. has no bearing on our impression of the horror of the scene. His fate is horrible in itself. Taylor makes T.J. an unlikeable character so that the reader's shock is uncomplicated by affection for the character. We do not like him and yet we still pity him.

Therefore T.J., desperate to be liked and to fit into the wider community, essentially stays the same while the events around him escalate. As Papa points out, somebody had to bear the brunt of the community's growing dissatisfaction. T.J. is never presented as intrinsically evil, he is merely weak and led astray by the white boys. As the last horrific scene explicitly demonstrates, there is a big gap between what happens to him and what he deserves. This means that in the end the disdain and small amount of pity we felt towards T.J. is transformed into a feeling of genuine sympathy.

The presentation of the character of T.J. is complex, and it can be seen from the discussion above that Taylor controls exactly the degree to which we feel sympathy for T.J., balancing and manipulating the reader's sensations of scorn, pity and sympathy.

---

(5) Connect at least three incidents from the action of the book to the specific moral messages that Cassie learns from her family.

Cassie's family are crucial in teaching her specific moral messages. These lessons result from parental discussion with Cassie when she has acted wrongly in particular situations, thus allowing her to apply the moral messages learned to future situations. Three incidents which illustrate this are: firstly, when Cassie learns from her family after the humiliating but formative day in Strawberry that sometimes you have to toe the line; secondly, the incident when she acts out her secret revenge on Lillian Jean; and thirdly, the incident when Cassie learns that her family is powerless to prevent T.J.'s fate. These incidents all inter-relate and help to form Cassie's intelligent moral nature, but they shall be treated separately here for simplicity of discussion.

When Cassie goes to Strawberry with Big Ma she is at first shocked that the white people have the prime position for their stalls in the market. This is because Cassie has been brought up with a feeling of equality and respect by her family. This later prompts her to believe that Mr Barnett has forgotten to serve them, and as a result she approaches Mr Barnett politely and reminds him of the order. T.J., in contrast, does not react to this example of prejudice because he has not been taught to value himself. Cassie is very angry when Barnett tells her that she should not return until she knows what she is. She shouts back at him, and is on the verge of telling him what she thinks he is, before she is finally thrown out of the store. This, together with her initial refusal to apologise to Lillian Jean, is proof of her belief in herself that has been nurtured by her parents. However she has to learn a new moral message from this incident. She has to learn to restrain her responses when she comes to the realisation that, although she is in the right, she is unable to combat the unfair advantage of the white community.

Later Cassie is talking to Papa on New Year's Day about 'whether or not Lillian Jean's worth taking a stand about' and Papa reminds her that if revenge is what she decides on, no one else must ever know. Cassie promises that Mr Simms will never hear about it as Cassie realises that if the adults got involved this could cause serious problems. She decides that this is something she has to do, and she goes about this in a calculated and private way, tricking Lillian Jean into thinking she is her friend and slave, and gaining her confidence. In fact Cassie uses the phrase 'we all gotta do what we gotta do' when she persuades Lillian Jean that she has changed. This is a phrase that Papa used when he was explaining to her about responsibility in Chapter 9. Ironically Lillian Jean chooses to misunderstand her. Cassie, having had her hair braided especially so that Lillian Jean cannot pull it, leads her up to the forest. She carefully hits Lillian Jean only where bruises will not be seen. At this point Cassie is only following some of the messages that her family have taught her. She has thought about her revenge and has not acted immediately, as Uncle Hammer would have. He is an example of the wrong kind of behavior When he runs off to find Mr Simms he could have caused trouble for whole family. Cassie never tells anyone about the incident, partly as a result of her discussion with Papa but also because she knows Mama would not approve. Her revenge on Lillian Jean is violent and she knows that according to Mama, it does not demand the respect that the Logans think they deserve.

The final incident which is connected to a specific moral message that Cassie learns from her family is in fact the final one of the novel: when Cassie realises that her family is powerless to prevent T.J.'s fate. Papa, by starting the fire, prevented T.J. from his immediate hanging but is unable to do anything more. What Cassie has to do this time is to accept that what happened to T.J. in the night will not pass. This acceptance and the tears that she sheds for T.J. and the land are symbols of her growth as a character and will affect her moral outlook for the rest of her life. She has had to confront the unfairness of the system of prejudice, as her parents before her had done, and still retain a feeling of equality. She must believe that she can choose what to make of her life, unlike T.J. who let society choose for him.

Therefore Cassie has to make choices and has to grow up during the course of the novel. The incidents discussed are only three of the important ones in the book. Each incident and specific moral message that Cassie learns from her family form the overall moral character of Cassie. Her choices are dictated by the moral atmosphere in which she grows up and the strength and support which her family give her.

---

(6) Is *Roll of Thunder, Hear My Cry* simply a novel about growing up?

Roll of Thunder, Hear My Cry is certainly a novel about growing up. All the Logan children are older and wiser by the end of the novel. Specific incidents mark the development of each child's character. For Stacey one of these incidents is when Hammer reproaches him for having given away the coat he got for Christmas. For Christopher-John, it is the moment in Chapter 12 in which he does not run after his siblings. Little Man, towards the end of the novel, stops being so obsessive about cleanliness. Cassie's development, however, occurs over a longer period of time and is not apparent by looking at one isolated incident, for she is the main character of the book about whom the wider issues of the novel revolve. It is her growing up on which we shall concentrate.

At the beginning of the novel Cassie is relatively ignorant of what it means to be black in the 1930s. The independence of her family and their relative wealth means that she has not had to confront 'how things are', as Miss Daisy Crocker describes the system of prejudice in operation at that time in the South. Although Cassie has accepted that the black children do not have a bus to take them to school, she cannot understand why Big Ma is allocated a bad position in the market, or why Mr Barnett and Mr

Simms treat her as an inferior being. She shares Little Man's outrage at the shoddy schoolbooks that the county has given them. Taylor creates a situation in which Cassie's state of ignorance is paralleled with the reader's ignorance, and simultaneously we have to learn about the hardship and oppression of black people.

Cassie learns through a number of incidents, for instance her trip to Strawberry with Big Ma and the situation regarding T.J. at the end of the novel. The learning processes which Cassie has to go through are often strongly presented, for instance the vision of the burned Mr Berry with his glittering eyes and charred face. When Mr Morrison embarks on his narrative of Christmas of seventy-six, when his family was murdered by night men, Mama protests that the story should not be told in the children's presence. However Papa tells her that the children need to know about the night men: 'It's their history.' Cassie's parents believe that learning about her history is an important part of her growing up. After Cassie has been humiliated in Strawberry by Mr Barnett, Lillian Jean and Mr Simms, Mama sits with her and explains about the history of slavery, and about why people behaved in the way that they did that day. Cassie has to understand that outside their house 'things are not always as we would have them to be'. Mama tells her that she has had to grow up a little. However she knows the limit of information appropriate to her child and in response to Cassie's question asking what will happen if 'Uncle Hammer gets to Mr Simms', Mama replies: 'I think you've done enough growing up for one day, Cassie.'

In the incidents examined above it can be seen that the issue of growing up is an important part of the novel. However, it is interesting to note that the incidents which make Cassie change and develop are largely concerned with issues of race. Growing up is important in itself, but growing up with a purpose – to learn to live in a racist society – is even more significant. This can be clearly seen in the final incident of the book where T.J. and his family are violently attacked by the white community. Cassie 'grows' as a result of this incident and she provides a strong focus to the novel. However, her growth is not the only message the author is trying to convey. The novel is about racial discrimination and aims to show that this discrimination is totally unjustifiable. This is shown in the same incidents which surround 'growing up', because it is by experiencing unfairness that the reader and the protagonists see the way things are in society.

As can be seen from the discussion above, the children's growing up is placed in a much larger context. The novel is not specifically about the relationship between parents and children, or about coming to terms with oneself. To describe *Roll of Thunder, Hear My Cry* as being 'simply a novel about growing up' therefore is limiting, and ignores the wider purpose of its author – that of the pressing issue of black consciousness that was at its peak at the time of writing.

Part 5

Suggestions for further reading

The text

TAYLOR, MILDRED D.: *Roll of Thunder, Hear My Cry*, Puffin Books, Harmondsworth, 1976.

Other works by Mildred D. Taylor

Song of the Trees, Dial Press, New York, 1975.
Let the Circle Be Unbroken, Puffin, London, 1982.
The Gold Cadillac, Bantam Press, New York, 1987.
The Friendship and other Stories, Heinemann New Windmills, Oxford, 1993.
The Road to Memphis, Penguin, London, 1992.

Background reading

Roll of Thunder, Hear My Cry has a niche in two recognisable genres. Firstly, it deals with the nature and processes of growing up. A selection of books concerned with this issue are:

DICKENS, CHARLES: *David Copperfield*, Penguin Classics, Penguin, 1966; reprinted 1985.
JOYCE, JAMES: *A Portrait of the Artist as a Young Man*, Twentieth Century Classics, Penguin, 1979.
RICHARDSON, HENRY HANDEL: *The Getting of Wisdom*, Heinemann, London, 1977.
SALINGER, J. D.: *The Catcher in the Rye*, Little, Brown, Boston, 1951. First published by Hamish Hamilton, London, 1951. The modern edition is published by Penguin Books and Hamish Hamilton, 1994.

The second important issue with which *Roll of Thunder, Hear My Cry* deals is the issue of racism. Novels that might be relevant when thinking about this include the following:

LEE, HARPER: *To Kill a Mockingbird*, Minerva, London, 1991.

MORRISON, TONI: *The Bluest Eye*, Picador, London, 1990.
WALKER, ALICE: *The Color Purple*, The Women's Press, London, 1983.

Critical studies

MARABLE, MANNING: *Race, Reform and Rebellion: The Second Reconstruction in Black America, 1945–1982*, Macmillan, London, 1984. The first chapter gives an impression of the racial situation in post Reconstruction U.S.A.
ALLT, A H.: *The American Civil War*, Longman, London, 1961.

The author of these notes

Laura Gray is a freelance writer who lives in Oxford. She was educated in Scotland, England and Italy.